Transactional Six Sigma for Green Belts

Maximizing Service and Manufacturing Processes

Also available from ASQ Quality Press:

Six Sigma for the Office: A Pocket Guide
Roderick A. Munro

Business Performance through Lean Six Sigma: Linking the Knowledge Worker, the Twelve Pillars, and Baldrige
James T. Schutta

The Certified Six Sigma Black Belt Handbook
Donald W. Benbow and T. M. Kubiak

Applied Data Analysis for Process Improvement: A Practical Guide to Six Sigma Black Belt Statistics
James L. Lamprecht

Applied Statistics for the Six Sigma Green Belt
Bhisham C. Gupta and H. Fred Walker

Six Sigma Project Management: A Pocket Guide
Jeffrey N. Lowenthal

Defining and Analyzing a Business Process: A Six Sigma Pocket Guide
Jeffrey N. Lowenthal

Six Sigma for the Next Millennium: A CSSBB Guidebook
Kim H. Pries

SPC for Right-Brain Thinkers: Process Control for Non-Statisticians
Lon Roberts

The Path to Profitable Measures: 10 Steps to Feedback That Fuels Performance
Mark W. Morgan

To request a complimentary catalog of ASQ Quality Press publications, call 800-248-1946, or visit our Web site at http://qualitypress.asq.org.

Transactional Six Sigma for Green Belts

Maximizing Service and Manufacturing Processes

Samuel E. Windsor

ASQ Quality Press
Milwaukee, Wisconsin

American Society for Quality, Quality Press, Milwaukee 53203
© 2006 by ASQ
All rights reserved. Published 2005
Printed in the United States of America

12 11 10 09 08 07 06 05   5 4 3 2 1

Library of Congress Cataloging-in-Publication Data

Windsor, Samuel E., 1962–
   Transactional Six Sigma for Green Belts : maximizing service and
manufacturing processes / Samuel E. Windsor.
     p. cm.
   Includes bibliographical references and index.
   ISBN-13: 978-0-87389-671-9 (soft cover : alk. paper)
   ISBN-10: 0-87389-671-8 (soft cover : alk. paper)
   1. Service industries—Management—Handbooks, manuals, etc.
2. Manufacturing processes—Management—Handbooks, manuals, etc.
3. Six sigma (Quality control standard)—Handbooks, manuals, etc. I. Title:
Maximizing service and manufacturing processes. II. Title.

   HD9980.65.W56 2005
   658.4'013—dc22
                                                 2005027494

ISBN-13: 978-0-87389-671-9
ISBN-10: 0-87389-671-8

Publisher: William A. Tony
Acquisitions Editor: Annemieke Hytinen
Project Editor: Paul O'Mara
Production Administrator: Randall Benson

ASQ Mission: The American Society for Quality advances individual,
organizational, and community excellence worldwide through learning,
quality improvement, and knowledge exchange.

Attention Bookstores, Wholesalers, Schools, and Corporations: ASQ Quality
Press books, videotapes, audiotapes, and software are available at quantity
discounts with bulk purchases for business, educational, or instructional use.
For information, please contact ASQ Quality Press at 800-248-1946, or write to
ASQ Quality Press, P.O. Box 3005, Milwaukee, WI 53201-3005.

To place orders or to request a free copy of the ASQ Quality Press Publications
Catalog, including ASQ membership information, call 800-248-1946. Visit our
Web site at www.asq.org or http://qualitypress.asq.org.

∞ Printed on acid-free paper

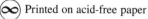

Quality Press
600 N. Plankinton Avenue
Milwaukee, Wisconsin 53203
Call toll free 800-248-1946
Fax 414-272-1734
www.asq.org
http://qualitypress.asq.org
http://standardsgroup.asq.org
E-mail: authors@asq.org

Contents

Preface

As I travel around the country teaching Six Sigma Green Belt and Black Belt courses, the most asked question is, "How does this apply to transactional processes?" Although the simple answer is that you can apply Six Sigma to any process, manufacturing or service, many students are not convinced at first. I think that the first thing the reader needs to understand, therefore, is exactly what I mean by *transactional Six Sigma*. In this text, *transactional* refers to any process where an actual product is not produced. Transactional processes are present everywhere, such as handling a customer complaint, taking an order at a fast-food restaurant, or processing a purchase order in a manufacturing company.

Transactional Six Sigma has come to be synonymous with the service sector, and normally focuses on a service that the customer sees. But it is important to understand that all businesses have transactional processes, both in the manufacturing sector and the service sector. The opportunity for improvement in processes that do not directly touch the product or service can be substantial.

Six Sigma, originally introduced in the manufacturing sector, is rapidly gaining the attention of many companies in the service sector. More and more, Six Sigma Green Belt and Black Belt classes contain a majority of students from health insurance providers, credit card companies, uniform service providers, and other service-related industries. In many cases, even the students from manufacturing companies bring transactional projects to class!

While experienced Six Sigma practitioners can clearly see the connection, Six Sigma trainees become confused and incorrectly conclude that Six Sigma really doesn't apply to them. In this book we will look at the tools that the Green Belt is expected to use, explain the purpose of the tool, and give examples that are designed to provoke thoughts of possible application for the mentioned tools. Once students understand that there is a measurable process involved in providing a service or transaction and they understand the tool, it becomes easier to apply Six Sigma to improve the process.

Think of this book as a home improvement–type book. Consider, for example, a book written on deck construction. The book may detail construction methods like setting posts and installing beams, but does not go into detail on the use of the hammer or screw gun. In my experience the confusion does not come from *how* to use a tool, but *when* to use that tool. Although we will cover each tool and discuss at a basic level how the tool works, I assume the reader has had at least some exposure to the tools available to the Green Belt.

The calculation examples contained in the text are not meant to replace a good statistical reference. The examples are meant to further the students' understanding of the tool. I have found that this assists the student in using the tools properly. In most cases the student will use a statistical software package. I have included references to the software package and, in some cases, Excel functions for data analysis. Although there are other excellent packages available, MINITAB is the one I am most familiar with.

Acknowledgments

The acknowledgments in most every book start out with something like, "No book is ever the work of one person." You really don't realize how true this is until you do it yourself. This book, like most others, is actually the work of many.

I first need to thank my good friend, neighbor, and fishing partner Edward Blackburn, who so diligently read and reread the manuscript and commented with "Huh?" when I had written sentences that made no sense. Ed would always provide candid feedback telling me what he didn't understand and offering suggestions for improvement.

I would also like to thank all of my Six Sigma students over the last few years who have helped me understand more by the questions they ask. One particular student, Becky Wampler, was always eager to read and comment from the point of view of a Six Sigma student and allowed her project to be used in this book.

A special thanks also goes to Biba Aidoo and Jill Gormley for their work that comprises the case study in Appendix A.

With the work that goes into such an undertaking, your family also pays a price. For this I thank my wife, Tammy, and son, Nicholas, for their patience and support.

1

Introduction

I f you ask someone to define *Six Sigma,* you will get about as
many answers as if you asked them to define *quality.* For the
purposes of this book, we will define *Six Sigma* as a method to
reduce process variation and control the centering of our process.

There are two critical items that people involved in service-
related Six Sigma projects must understand in order for this definition to be meaningful. The first is that you must think of what you
do in terms of a process. Everything is a process, from getting to
work in the morning to waiting on a bank customer at the bank
teller's window. The second crucial item is that you must have a
method to measure the output or performance of the process. The
measurement may be in terms of dollars, time, or some sort of customer satisfaction rating, but there must be a measure. Once we
understand that we actually have a process and that we can measure
the process, we are well on the way to understanding the application
of Six Sigma in a transactional environment.

As simple as this sounds, without practical examples and an
understanding of each tool, Six Sigma can become very difficult to
apply. Think of Six Sigma much like the toolbox you have at home.
There are many tools, some you use often and many less often. There
are also many times when you could use any one of several tools to
do the same job. Say, for example, you need to tighten a bolt on
little Sally's bike. You could use an adjustable wrench, a socket
and ratchet, or a combination wrench. Each tool has advantages and

disadvantages, but any would work in this situation. This is really no different than having a Six Sigma toolbox with a *t*-test and ANOVA inside. In some cases either would do the job just fine.

The difficult part for a Green Belt in training is learning when to apply what tool. This is especially true in the service sector where one is much less likely to have used any of these tools in the past. One advantage that manufacturing Green Belts have over service sector Green Belts is that the tools have been in use for quite a while on the manufacturing side. Many people in banking, healthcare, and other nonmanufacturing environments have never heard of process capability much less calculated it. A flowchart of a typical Green Belt Six Sigma project is shown in Figure 1.1.

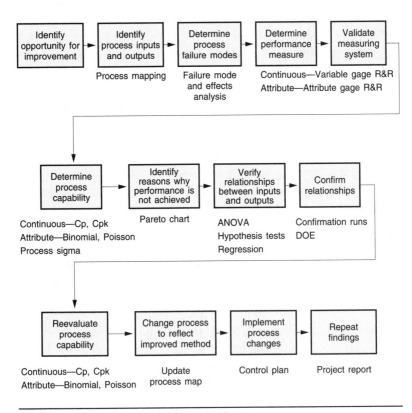

Figure 1.1 Green Belt Six Sigma project process map.

In Six Sigma, process capability is what it is all about. A Six Sigma process produces about 3.4 defects per million, which is about one defect or mistake in every 294,117 transactions. There are really only two ways to improve process capability. One is to reduce variation and the other is to move the process average closer to the target. Thus, our definition of reducing variation and centering the process. In many Six Sigma projects the actual defect rate of 3.4 parts per million (ppm) may never be achieved, but this does not mean the project was a failure. It is far more important to improve the process to the point where it consistently meets the requirements of the customer rather than meeting a standard target of 3.4 defects per million. There will be times when 3.4 defects per million is not a realistic goal and other times when 3.4 defects per million is unacceptable performance, for example in airline travel.

Our goal when we embark on a Six Sigma project is to bring the average of the process as close to the target (what the customer requires) with the least amount of variation as possible. We accomplish this by understanding the process and relating the process inputs to the process outputs and then controlling the inputs in such a way that the outcome is predictable. For example, if you are a customer of a large bank and you expect it to take 20 minutes to open an account, you would always expect the time to be around 20 minutes, even if you were to open five accounts at different times. Any more than 20 minutes and you may be late for your next appointment; any less time and you may feel that the bank was rushing you. The variation we must investigate is the time differences between the five visits. The target is how well the bank performed to the expectation of 20 minutes. Given this information we need to understand all the factors that contribute to the transaction taking either more or less time than anticipated. When those factors are understood and their relationship defined, the output will become predictable and controllable.

The process of Six Sigma involves knowing the expectations of the customer, measuring your performance to those expectations, and acting on the results of that measurement in order to meet the customer expectations. Six Sigma employs the process of *define, measure, analyze, improve, and control* (DMAIC) to accomplish this. For the Green Belt, the assigned project should have already been defined by the management team, which means that the problem is stated and the objective given. For example, management may say, "Customer satisfaction is 4 on a scale of 1 to 10, and by the end of the year it should be at least 7." In this text we will not be concerned with the define project phase, our focus will be on the measure, analyze, improve, and control phases. In each phase it is important to understand what we are trying to accomplish and understand what tools are available. We will focus on what tool to use for a particular task and briefly cover its application.

DEFINE

Although the Green Belt is typically not involved in the define stage of Six Sigma, it is important to recognize that this stage is the basis for a successful project. Projects are selected at the executive and champion level and are tied directly to the business needs. Projects are prioritized by the level of pain to the organization. By *pain,* we are referring to the impact on cost, quality, or delivery of the product or service. Six Sigma projects need to be focused on a particular process or service and be achievable in four to six months. Six Sigma projects are *not* the following:

1. Install new computer system.

2. Implement new claims process.

3. Develop new business opportunity.

Installing a new computer system or implementing a new claims process are projects and may be important to the company, but they are not Six Sigma projects. They may be the result of another project, but are not Six Sigma projects within themselves. Six Sigma projects are meant to be a process by which a defined problem is measured, analyzed (investigated), improved, and controlled. If the decision has already been made to upgrade a computer or change a process, there is no need to apply the Six Sigma tools.

Examples of Six Sigma projects are as follows:

1. Reduce the number of overpaid claims by 50% in six months.

2. Reduce process cycle time by 30%.

3. Increase employee retention rate to 95%.

4. Reduce the cycle time of installing new computers by 50%.

These examples all address a process that must be improved and set a goal for that improvement. The fourth item, reduce the cycle time of installing new computers by 50%, may not seem very different from item 1 in the first example, install new computer system, but they are. Installing a new computer system is the output of a decision that has already been made and is a one-time project. Reducing the cycle time of installing a new computer system relates to improving the ongoing process of installing computer systems.

Project Focus

It is important to select a project that has focus. While it would be nice to think that a Six Sigma student could, after training, "improve customer satisfaction by 50%," a project like this may not be possible. A measurement like customer satisfaction is made of many components and subprocesses. Six Sigma instructors call this a "boil the ocean" or "end world hunger" project. Although stretch goals are good, a Six Sigma project must be achievable in a reasonable period of time and must be within the capability of the Six Sigma candidate. Most projects that students bring to class require the focus to be narrowed to a process that contributes to the overall goal, say customer satisfaction at one location or for one type of service.

MEASURE

In the second phase, measure, we are attempting to understand how well the process is performing to the intended goal or specification. The two parts of this equation are the specification or requirement from the customer (be it an internal or external customer) and the current process performance. We will refer to this as *process capability.*

ANALYZE

Once the relationship between process performance and customer expectation is understood and the gaps identified, we can begin to understand how the process inputs relate to the process outputs with respect to process centering and process variation. We do this in the analyze phase. In this phase, tools such as analysis of variance (ANOVA), hypothesis testing, and regression will be used.

IMPROVE

In the improve phase, we take this analysis a little further by changing the process inputs in order to determine the effect on and optimize the outputs. This will be done through a series of controlled experiments called design of experiments (DOE).

CONTROL

The final stage of process improvement is the control phase. This is where the known relationships between inputs and outputs are defined, documented, and made a permanent part of the process. This is the step where actions are taken to hold the gains made in the project.

As a Green Belt you may be asked to lead a team or be part of a larger team. This will involve conducting and managing meetings, keeping the team on track, and documenting team results.

In the following chapters, we will explore each tool and give examples of the application of each tool in detail. We will use the example of driving to work in the morning to make the application of the tools as straightforward as possible. The example is not meant to be serious, but a lighthearted example that I have found useful in conducting training over the years. At the end of the discussion of each tool, several examples of real-world transaction processes will be given. While not an all-inclusive list, the goal is to present sufficient ideas to start the process of applying the tools to your individual project.

EXAMPLE PROJECT

Management has determined that our arrival time to work does not meet the target and is highly variable. We are required to arrive at work between 7:45 AM and 8:00 AM daily. If we arrive early, we have to stand outside until the building opens. If we are late, we are not available to perform work.

In this case, the customer specification is that we are available at work by 8:00 AM. So in this case the process measure will be arrival time. In the next chapter we continue by understanding the process through process mapping and failure mode and effects analysis (FMEA). This example project will be included along with other real-world examples throughout the text as those topics are discussed. The examples may seem to jump around because I have attempted to show as many applications of the tool being discussed as possible. The examples are meant to provoke a thought as to a possible application of the tool. Table 1.1 lists potential projects and the related process measures.

Table 1.1   Potential projects, measures, and goals to consider.

Project	Measure	Goal
Purchase order process	Days/hours to complete	Approve POs in 24 hours or less.
Handling customer complaints	Time to resolution/ satisfaction of customer with outcome	Resolve customer complaints in 48 hours with a satisfaction average rating of 9 on a scale of 1–10.
Healthcare claim payment accuracy	Dollars over/under target payment amount	Pay all claims within 5% of target payment.
Customer returns	Accuracy of return classification	Improve classification accuracy to 99%.
Warranty claims	Amount paid versus amount required to be paid	Improve claim payment measure to less than 1%.
Employee turnover rate	Percent monthly turnover	Reduce turnover by 50%.

Key Points

1. Six Sigma is about centering the process on target and reducing variation.

2. Think of everything as a process.

3. Understand what the customer requires.

4. Determine how the output is measured.

5. A measurable improvement goal must be specified.

CHAPTER REFERENCES

Harry, Mikel J. *Six Sigma Breakthrough Management Strategy.* New York: Doubleday, 2000.

———. *The Vision of Six Sigma.* Phoenix: Tri Star Publishing, 1997.

2

The Tools

T he tools of Six Sigma are deeply rooted in the basic tools of quality, which have been in use for many years. Although this text is not meant as a guide to the basic tools of quality, sometimes called the seven tools of quality, the tools are worth discussing. The traditional seven tools are as follows:

1. Checklist

2. Pareto chart

3. Flowchart

4. Cause-and-effect diagram

5. Histogram

6. Scatter diagram

7. Control chart/run chart

Each of the tools will be used in a Six Sigma project in one form or another. When learning the DMAIC process, many students begin to think of the improvement process as only sequential and struggle to understand where a tool like the cause-and-effect diagram fits in. The truth is that many of the basic tools can be used several times at various points in the improvement process. In this section, we will investigate the use and purpose of each of the basic quality tools with the goal of understanding when to apply each.

CHECKLIST

Checklist sheets are simple tools designed to allow one to organize observations in a meaningful manner. Using a checklist sheet can be as simple as recording the number of times a particular problem occurs. Checklists are used to collect data over a period of time in order to determine what the most significant contributor to the problem is. Without a tool like a checklist, it is very difficult to determine what the most frequently occurring problem is over a period of time. If you were to ask workers what their most commonly occurring issue is, they could most likely tell you the most recent issue but not the most frequently occurring issue.

PARETO CHART

The Pareto chart is a simple and powerful tool to graphically indicate how different categories of failure modes contribute to an issue under investigation. If data were collected over a period of time of reasons for customer returns, a Pareto chart of that data would look like Figure 2.1

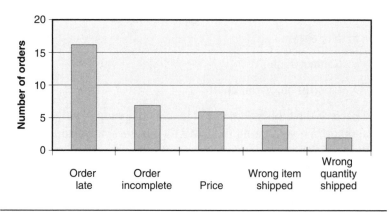

Figure 2.1 Sample Pareto chart of customer complaints.

The concept of the Pareto principle is that 80% of problems come from 20% of the causes, also referred to as the 80/20 rule. The exact numbers are not important, but the idea is a useful method in applying resources to solve a problem. If we start with the idea that it is easier to reduce a problem by 50% than it would be to eliminate it altogether, we see that reducing the number of late orders in Figure 2.1 by 50% would result in a reduction of 8 defects (half of 16), which would be a greater overall improvement than completely eliminating failures for wrong item shipped and wrong quantity shipped, which would only give a total defect reduction of 6.

A Pareto chart is generated by graphing the number of occurrences of a particular failure mode in descending order. The Pareto chart is useful any time process failure or defects can have a number of causes. Use of the Pareto chart will allow you to determine the most frequent cause of a process failure and help direct resources to resolve that problem.

As demonstrated in Figure 2.2, Pareto charts can also be used to identify the largest source of input to a process. Figure 2.2 lists the numbers of claims by location (locations are identified as numbers 1–5). In this case, claim locations 3 and 2 produce the highest number of claims that must be processed.

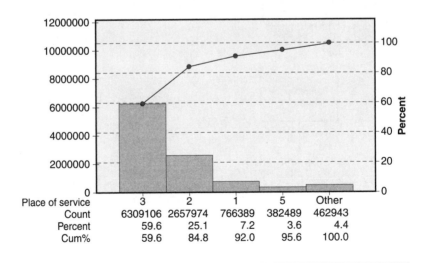

Place of service	3	2	1	5	Other
Count	6309106	2657974	766389	382489	462943
Percent	59.6	25.1	7.2	3.6	4.4
Cum%	59.6	84.8	92.0	95.6	100.0

Figure 2.2   Pareto of January–June 2004 claims by location.

FLOWCHART

The process map used in Six Sigma is really a variant of a flow-chart. The flowchart in its more traditional application employs different shapes of boxes to represent different activities. The flowchart is used to understand the flow of a process and is useful for identifying disconnects and non-value-added steps. Some of the standard flowchart shapes are shown in Figure 2.3. A simple flowchart for a procurement process may look like Figure 2.4.

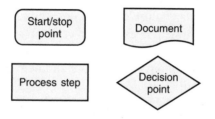

Figure 2.3 Sample flowchart symbols.

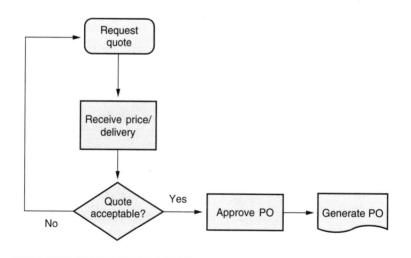

Figure 2.4 Sample procurement process flowchart.

CAUSE-AND-EFFECT DIAGRAM

The cause-and-effect diagram, as shown in Figure 2.5, also known as an Ishikawa diagram or fishbone diagram, is used to identify potential causes of a given effect. The diagram is typically used in a team brainstorming setting where ideas are presented in a round-robin fashion. The purpose of the diagram and brainstorming exercise is to gather as many potential causes of the given problem as possible. Comments are held until the team has exhausted all ideas and recorded them on the chart. The causes are prioritized by voting or another method to identify the most relevant causes according to the team. Those causes are recorded for further investigation by the team.

Potential causes are grouped into one of six categories, called the Six Ms. There are many variations of the categories used for the diagram such as man (people), method, materials, machine, Mother Nature (environment), and measurement. Categories such as policies/procedures, people, equipment, and process could also be used. The categories are used as an aid to help group members organize their thoughts and include all potential failure modes. A completed cause-and-effect diagram is shown in Figure 2.6.

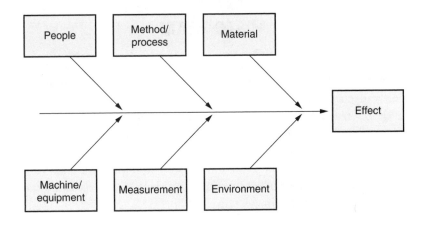

Figure 2.5 Cause-and-effect categories.

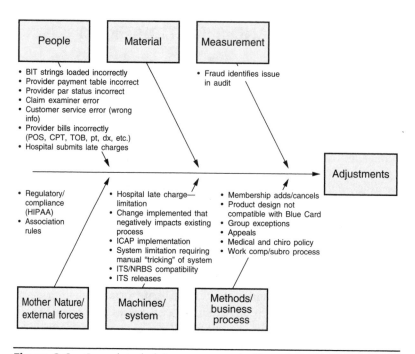

Figure 2.6   Completed claims cause-and-effect diagram.

HISTOGRAM

The histogram, as shown in Figure 2.7, is a tool used to graphically represent continuous data. The histogram "bins" the data into several data ranges. Typically the range of data is divided into 10 to 15 bins of equal size. When data are plotted on a histogram, it becomes very easy to see the shape of the distribution. Understanding the shape of the distribution is very critical when analyzing data. You should always look at the shape of the data before attempting to analyze it. Just a look at the data in a histogram can identify outliers and other data points that do not make sense.

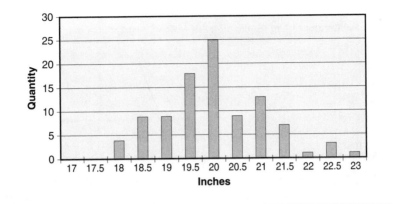

Figure 2.7   Sample histogram.

SCATTER DIAGRAM

The scatter diagram, as shown in Figure 2.8, is a useful tool for comparing any continuous input to a continuous output to determine how the output changes as the input changes. The diagram is a plot of the input variable on the x-axis with the corresponding output on the y-axis. In later chapters the scatter diagram will be used with correlation and regression to validate the relationship and to develop a regression equation used to predict the output at a given input level.

The sample scatter diagram in Figure 2.8 compares the average number of applications received to the average number of applications processed per day. It was generated in MINITAB but could have been done in Excel or even manually. The graph indicates that as the number of application receipts increases, so does the number of applications processed.

CONTROL CHART/RUN CHART

A run chart, as shown in Figure 2.9, is used any time we want to investigate what happens over time. Run charts come in various formats and are commonly used as the tool to track process performance during a Six Sigma project.

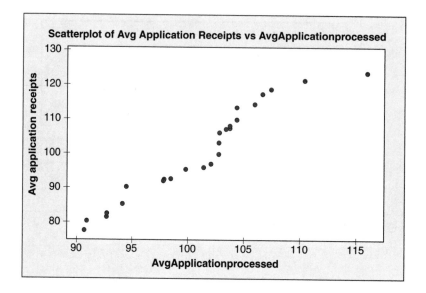

Figure 2.8

Figure 2.8 A scatter diagram created in MINITAB showing the number of applications received in a given time period compared to the number of applications processed in that time period.

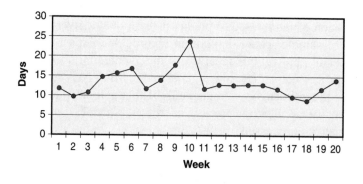

Figure 2.9 Run chart of the average cycle time for orders closed in a given week.

The control chart is really an expansion of a run chart with the addition of *control limits*. See Figure 2.10 for an example. There are many types of control charts and their use is largely determined by the type of process you wish to monitor. Controls charts will be discussed in further detail in the control phase of this text.

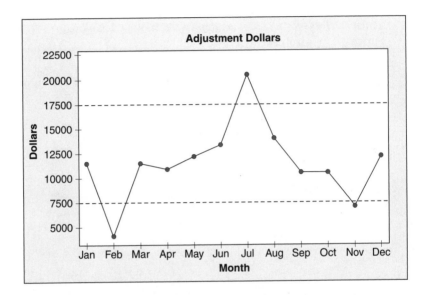

Figure 2.10 Run chart generated in MINITAB showing claims adjustment dollars per month.

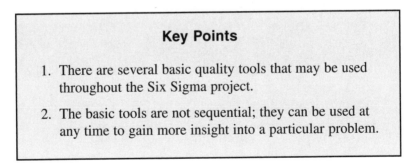

Key Points

1. There are several basic quality tools that may be used throughout the Six Sigma project.

2. The basic tools are not sequential; they can be used at any time to gain more insight into a particular problem.

CHAPTER REFERENCES

Boeing. *Advanced Quality System Tools*. D1-9000-1. November 1998. http://www.isixsigma.com/tt/.

Juran, Joseph M., and A. Blanton Godfrey. *Juran's Quality Handbook*. 5th ed. New York: McGraw-Hill, 1999.

Kiemele, Mark J., Stephen R. Schmidt, and Ronald J. Berbine. *Basic Statistics, Tools for Continuous Improvement*. 4th ed. Colorado Springs, CO: Air Academy Press, 2000.

3

Teams

Much has been written about teams, team building, and improving team performance. Teams are important in getting the most from a Six Sigma project, as many projects are cross-functional and require cooperation from many different areas of a business. The intention of this chapter is to provide a brief overview of the concepts relating to teams that the Green Belt should be aware of.

Although not considered a tool, teams are a critical element in most any Six Sigma project. Most projects are assigned and the team given a charter from a sponsor or *champion,* as they are called in Six Sigma. The charter defines the objective of the team, scope of the work to be performed, membership, and resources allocated to the team. The purpose the charter is to get the team started, provide some direction without solving the problem, and to keep the team focused throughout the project. The charter defines the first of several items required for a team to be successful, a clear description of what needs to be accomplished.

In this text the focus will be on short-term project teams, as many projects will have duration of around three to six months, after which the team will be disbanded. Teams for Six Sigma projects should consist of representatives from the areas that will be affected by the project, someone with Six Sigma experience, and a financial representative to validate the results of the team. It is always tricky deciding who should be on a project team. A good team is made up of different types of people who can work well together. Collectively the team must have the ability to plan, organize, and complete work within a given schedule. The team members need to learn and apply new techniques quickly and not be upset by setbacks that they will most likely encounter. As a team is brought together, it is said that it goes through four stages:

1. Forming

2. Storming

3. Norming

4. Performing

In the forming stage, the team members are new and not completely sure of what is required or how they fit in on the team. At this stage it is important to clearly define the purpose of the team, set the code of conduct for the meetings and team interactions, and define each team member's role. The team is typically easy to manage in this stage because even though the team members may be a little anxious about the new team experience, they want to participate.

The second stage of the team, which will begin to happen after a few meetings, is called storming. Many teams, if not properly managed, will not make it through this stage. In the storming stage, team members have become comfortable with each other and are becoming more open about expressing their views. While in a fully developed team this is what you are trying achieve, in a new team without established roles, confrontation and individualism will quickly destroy the team atmosphere. It is important that the team recognize that this stage will pass and stay focused on the team's objective.

Stage three, norming, is the stage where everything starts to come together and the team begins to gel. Conflicts between team members are reduced and people become focused on the goal of the team and not individual achievement.

Stage four, performing, is the reward for making it through stage two and stage three. Here, the team has matured, has a clear focus on the purpose of the team, and its members get a sense of satisfaction from the team's achievements.

As with any group, the project team needs a designated leader. Decisions will be made collectively, but there has to be a key person to keep the team focused on the objective. Without a good leader the team will be doomed to almost certain failure. The leader's role is to:

1. Clarify the objective of the team.

2. Ensure there is an agenda and that it is adhered to.

3. Manage the action item list.

4. Guide the team through the problem-solving process.

5. Access the team's performance to plan.

6. Encourage and support the team.

7. Plan the team's next meeting and agenda.

The team leader must also decide on the type and level of training the team requires. The team may require very basic team training if it is made up of a group that has very little experience working as a team. The team will also require at least some training relating to the Six Sigma tools. For example, it will be very difficult to have an effective cause-and-effect brainstorming session if the participants do not understand the brainstorming and cause-and-effect process. The level of training should be tailored to what is asked of the team member. Although it would be nice if everyone were trained in all aspects of Six Sigma, it is just not practical or required for most projects. In many cases the Green Belt will be the team leader and will have to train the team members enough to understand the basic use and purpose of the tools.

One of the most important tools a team leader can have is the action item list. See Figure 3.1. The action item list serves as both a to-do list and a record of completed tasks. The action item list states the task requiring completion, who is responsible, a description of current activity and the target completion date, and any other information required to describe the action required. The action item list should be reviewed and updated at every team meeting. The results of team discussion and questions will provide additional action items for the team members to complete.

Owner: Terri
Team members: Mary, John, Joe, Sue, Tammy, Jim, Terri

Item status	Issue origination date	Item originator	Description	Person responsible	Current activity	Target date
Open	Apr 10	John	Complete Pareto chart of complaints	Mary	Collecting data	4-27
Open	Apr 11	Mary	Collect data for cycle time ANOVA	Joe	Waiting for report to be completed	4-21
Open	Apr 14	Sue	Install analysis software on team members' computers	Jim	Software due 4-18	4-21
Closed	Apr 1	Terri	Meet with champion to discuss performance measure	Tammy	Complete	4-9

Figure 3.1   Sample action item list.

Key Points

1. Teams are a critical part of successfully completing a Six Sigma project.

2. Teams must pass four milestones to be effective: forming, storming, norming, and performing.

3. The Green Belt may have to train their project team in basic Six Sigma tools.

CHAPTER REFERENCES

Avery, Christopher. "How Teamwork Can Be Developed As an Individual Skill." *Journal for Quality & Participation* 3, no. 24 (Fall 2000).

Guttman, Howard M. "Effective White-Collar Teams." *Quality Progress* 37, no. 6 (June 2004): 24.

Juran, Joseph M., and A. Blanton Godfrey. *Juran's Quality Handbook.* 5th ed. New York: McGraw-Hill, 1999.

Quality Council of Indiana. *Six Sigma Black Belt Primer.* Terre Haute, IN: Quality Council of Indiana, 2001.

4

Process Understanding

PROCESS MAPPING

The first step in a Six Sigma project, once the team is assembled, is to map and understand the process. This step is called process mapping. The process will be depicted as a series of blocks connected by lines showing the flow of the transaction through the process. Each process step will be given its own block in the process map. See Figure 4.1. After the process map is assembled we will dive deeper into our understanding by using a tool known as failure mode and effects analysis (FMEA).

Process inputs and outputs will also be identified for each step in the process. Each process step is an activity. Everything that an activity requires for successful execution is considered an input. The process outputs will be the measurable outcomes of each process

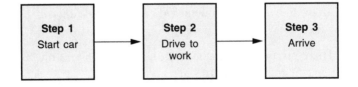

Figure 4.1 Example of process map format from the drive to work project.

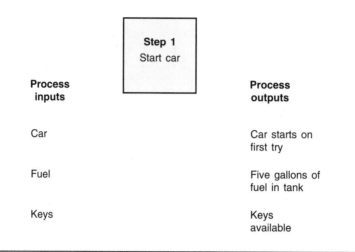

Figure 4.2   Simple process map with inputs and outputs identified.

step. See Figure 4.2. Process inputs and outputs are then identified for each of the remaining steps.

By understanding a process map and its purpose on a basic level, it becomes easier to apply the tool to a more complex example. Two additional process map examples follow. The first relates to the process of finding and hiring employees. It was done for a company that suspected that its hiring process contributed to a high turnover rate. See Figure 4.3. The second process map was taken from a large processor of healthcare claims and was developed to address a high rate of claims adjustments. See Figure 4.4.

The process mapping exercise is worth the effort and may take much longer than expected. Those involved with the process assume that they know and understand the process. When sufficient time is spent on this stage, however, most team members will find there are several steps that are not understood. Typical findings in process mapping are:

1. There are process disconnects, especially where multiple departments or locations are involved.

2. Responsibilities are not consistently defined.

3. There are process steps that rely on individuals recognizing potential problems.

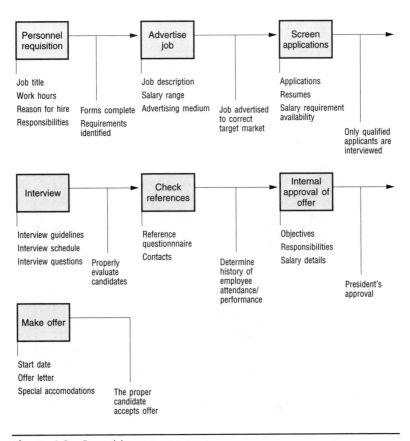

Figure 4.3 Recruiting process map.

4. There are process steps that no one is really sure why they are required. These are typically a holdover from the way things used to be.

5. There are process inputs not relating to process outputs. (This can be a result of the process changing over time and a particular input is no longer required.)

The major goal of the process map is to understand the flow of the process and how the steps relate to each other so team members can begin to understand the relationship of the key process input variables (KPIV) to the key process output variables (KPOV). The inputs are what is required for each process step and the output is

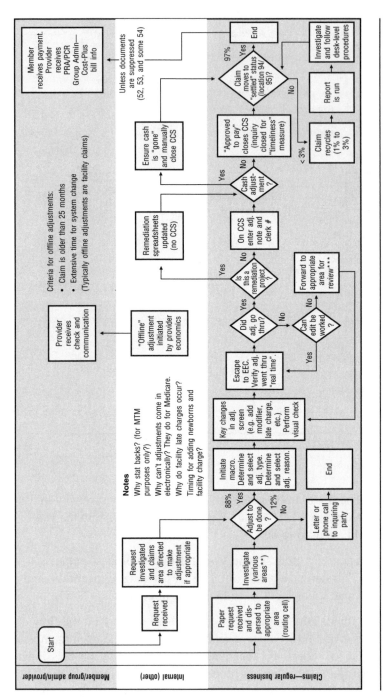

Figure 4.4 Sample healthcare claims process map.

the measurable outputs of each step. On the surface, measurable outputs of transactional processes may not be evident. It helps to think of how each step contributes to either quality, cost, or cycle time of the process. When that relationship is made, the measurable output is much easier to determine. In our drive to work example, we have an input of a car. How do we measure the performance of the car as it relates to the process of getting to work? In this case the important factor was that the car started on the first try, something we can measure.

FAILURE MODE AND EFFECTS ANALYSIS

At this point the process has been identified, all steps have been recorded, and inputs and outputs identified. The next step in the journey consists of taking each process step and investigating every input to determine what can go wrong, how likely it is to go wrong, what is the chance of detecting it if it does go wrong, and how much it affects the processes if it does go wrong. Analyzing the process steps like this is called failure mode and effects analysis (FMEA).

The purpose of FMEA is to rank the failure modes in order of importance so that resources can be applied to address the most critical issues first. We do this by rating the chance that something will happen (occurrence), how much it will impact the process if it does go wrong (severity), and how likely we are to detect that it will happen before it affects the process (detection). Each is rated from 1 to 10 with a 10 having the most adverse impact on the process. The actual values of the ratings will vary by process and company. The three ratings are multiplied together to form what is called a risk priority number (RPN). Items with the highest RPN are addressed first in the process improvement effort. See Table 4.1.

Table 4.2 is an FMEA for our drive to work example. From this example we see that the first item we will apply resources to will be the keys, since it has the highest RPN. This exercise not only helps us think through the process with a focus on what can go wrong, it will serve as a method to identify the easy solutions for quick improvements. The FMEA will also serve as a checklist of inputs and outputs from investigation in later stages of the project. Table 4.3 is another example of a completed FMEA.

Table 4.1   FMEA ratings.

Rating	Severity	Occurrence	Detection
1	No impact	Very unlikely, 1 in 1,000,000 or less	Can easily detect
2	Very minor impact	1 in 100,000	Almost certain
3	Minor impact	1 in 10,000	Very high chance of detection
4	Slight impact	1 in 1000	High chance of detection
5	Low impact	1%	Moderately high chance of detection
6	Moderate impact	3%	Moderate chance of detection
7	High impact	5%	Moderately low chance of detection
8	Very high impact	10%	Low chance of detection
9	Sever impact with warning	30%	Very low chance of detecting
10	Severe without warning	Very likely, 50% or more	Impossible to detect

Table 4.2   Drive to work FMEA.

Process Step	Failure Mode	Occurrence	Detection	Severity	RPN $O \times D \times S$
Start car	Car will not start.	2	8	9	216
Car	Battery is dead.	2	8	9	144
Fuel	There's less fuel than required.	3	2	3	18
Keys	Keys are locked in house.	4	8	9	288

Table 4.3 Example healthcare claims processing FMEA addressing claims adjustments.

Process	Failure Mode	Failure Effects	SEV	Causes	OCC	Controls	DET	RPN	Action Recommended	Responsible Person
Claims adjudi-cation	Provider submits incorrect informa-tion (diagnosis, CPT, provider number, patient name, etc.).	Claim must be adjusted.	10	Incorrect information received from provider.	4	Verification of provider number, patient number, sex, etc. Not failproof—dependent upon info received.	10	400	1) Internal education to ensure clerks are validating information or seeking out more current information when appropriate. 2) Provider education.	1) Claims training 2) Provider relations reps
	Provider submits additional charges.	Claim must be adjusted.	10	Additional healthcare services are rendered.	2	Contractually required to accept.	10	200	Provider education	Provider relations staff Provider comm staff
	Member is not on membership file.	Claim must be adjusted.	10	Group allowed retroactive add/term date. Or newborn not added timely.	2	Try to limit retro additions and cancellations to no more than 60 days.	9	180	Group education/ sales education	Group enrollment team
	Member has other coverage (coordi-nation of benefits).	Claim must be adjusted.	10	Spouse has coverage.	2	Query members regularly for other coverage.	6	120	Member application/ member communications	Field sales staff—completion of application Member communi-cation area
	Member benefits are loaded incorrectly.	Claim must be adjusted.	10	Coding error.	1	QA process.	10	100	Need to verify accuracy of benefit file coding.	Benefit implemen-tation team Customer service

Many teams get hung up on the actual ratings they assign, but what is important is that a consistent method is used for ranking the items. Remember, this is a tool to prioritize improvement activities.

A word of caution concerning ratings: Be aware of liability issues or standard ratings your company may use. You would not want to be in a situation where you said something was likely to occur, would occur without warning, and would be hazardous and you did nothing about it. Teams may set a minimum RPN value at which it is agreed upon that any item with an RPN below this value will not require further action.

ASK "WHY?" FIVE TIMES

A popular statement you may have heard is, "Ask *why* five times." This is intended to assist you in getting to the root cause of a problem. The thinking is that if you can drill down through at least five layers of causes, you can identify the true cause of a problem and react to it rather than just reacting to a symptom of the problem. In many cases you will find you may have to ask why six to 10 times to find the real root cause.

As an example, say a customer does not know about a new service offered by a local bank.

Q1. Why didn't the customer know?

A1. Teller was not aware of the available services.

Q2. Why was the teller not aware?

A2. New services were not communicated to tellers.

Q3. Why was the service not communicated to tellers?

A3. Branch manager was not aware of new service.

Q4. Why was the branch manager not aware?

A4. Literature describing new service did not arrive.

Q5. What happened to the literature?

A5. Literature was not ordered in time.

Q6. Why was the literature not ordered?

A6. Program was launched with insufficient lead time due to competition.

In this example, it seems that the customer was not offered the new service due to the fact that the teller was not aware a service was available. The *real* cause of the problem was that the literature lead time was greater than the lead time to launch a new program. The program was launched and the literature designed to explain the program to the bank employees was not available. In this case the problem does not lie with the teller or branch manager, but with reducing the cycle time to distribute literature communicating new services.

Key Points

1. Process mapping and FMEA are tools to help understand the process.

2. The process map lists the steps of a process; the inputs are what the process step requires; the process outputs are what is produced by the process step.

3. Time and care should be taken in process mapping so that everyone understands what really happens in the process and does not depend on what they think they know. Remember, if you really knew the answers, the problem would have been solved by now.

4. Ask *why* at least five times to determine the true root cause of a problem.

CHAPTER REFERENCES

Ireson, W. Grant. *Handbook of Reliability Engineering and Management.* 2nd ed. New York: McGraw-Hill, 1996.

Juran, Joseph M., and A. Blanton Godfrey. *Juran's Quality Handbook.* 5th ed. New York: McGraw-Hill, 1999.

Quality Council of Indiana. *CSSBB Primer.* Terre Haute, IN: Quality Council of Indiana, 2001.

5

Process Measures

Perhaps the most difficult part of using Six Sigma in a service or transactional environment is measuring the performance of the process. Having decided that everything we do is, in fact, a process, the next step is to determine how we will measure performance of our process. We should start with the key measures for any business, which are quality, cost, and cycle time. If the assigned project does not address at least one of these keys measures, the validity of the project should be questioned.

Measuring performance is the stage at which manufacturing and transactional projects may become different. In the manufacturing world you have direct measurements, like length, weight, or some other performance measure. In the transactional world, many things are important but may not be measured. For example, a key transactional measure is cycle time, that is, how long it will take a given transaction to pass through the process. Specific cycle times could be, how long does it take to pay a healthcare claim? Or, how long does it take to process a loan application? Or in our earlier example, how long does it take to get to work?

Another metric to consider in a transactional process is the cost. For example, if your process issues credits to a customer or gives discounts, are you properly applying the discounts? Say a credit is issued for $100 and the amount should have been $50. That becomes a cost variance of $50, a potential metric for a Six Sigma project.

Table 5.1 Examples of processes and potential process measures.

Process	Process Measure
Generating purchase orders	Cycle time in hours
HR recruitment process	Open positions
Supplier performance	On-time delivery
Supplier quality improvement project	Supplier acceptance rate
Healthcare claims process	Dollars paid over requirement
Sales order entry process	Cycle time in hours
Consulting company	Profit per project
Internal IT help desk	Satisfaction with service
Report publishing	Errors per report

The next consideration is what type of data will be collected. Will it be data that could be considered continuous, such as time or dollars, or will it be attribute/discrete data, such as percent defective or defects per unit? Whatever data are collected, they should reflect a measurable and controllable output of the process. The goal of the Six Sigma project is to determine how the outputs are affected by the inputs, so you can get to the point where the inputs are controlled and the output is predictable. This requires a good measure of process performance and an understanding of the relationship of the process inputs to the process outputs. With a little thought and focus on what is important to the customer and the process, meaningful measures can be created. See Table 5.1.

COST OF POOR QUALITY

The cost of quality or cost of poor quality is meant to capture any cost that is associated with a process failure. The cost of quality includes four major categories:

1. *Internal failure.* Costs associated with internal process breakdowns, including rework and scrap.

2. *External failure.* Costs associated with customer returns, complaints, recalls, and field failures.

3. *Appraisal.* The cost to evaluate, inspect, or measure a process, product, or service.

4. *Prevention.* Costs incurred by training, education, and systems to prevent errors.

Quality costs have been identified and measured for years within quality organizations with varying degrees of success. Arguably, the concept of quality costs is as important as actually measuring the true cost of poor quality. Many quality costs are difficult, if not impossible, to measure and have long been a point of contention between quality and accounting groups within organizations. Take, for example, external failure costs, which include customer dissatisfaction. How can the cost of lost business be accurately captured? The simple answer is that it is difficult to measure and almost impossible to accurately capture. It is important to realize, though, that such things do have a cost to the organization. In fact, any time a product or service has to be re-touched or reprocessed there is a cost associated with it. Many companies have complete customer service organizations to handle customer complaints and process failures. If a product or service was delivered perfectly and completely documented to the point where every customer question was already answered, many of the toll-free customer service numbers could be eliminated. In the case of the auto industry, if cars were delivered perfect every time, there would be little need for dealer service other than routine maintenance.

Six Sigma focuses on keeping processes on target and reducing variation to the point where the processes become predictable and deliver products of very high quality that require little or no additional resources to maintain. This also applies to internal processes. Think of verification or approval steps in a process; what is the real purpose? The real purpose of verification is to detect (or inspect) for some sort of error or oversight. What if the process could be designed and controlled to the point where errors could not occur? How many of the verification and approval steps could be eliminated? After all, verification and approval are just another name for inspection. How much could be saved in terms of cost and cycle time without the addition of non-value-added inspection steps? This is an area where many transactional or service processes have a huge opportunity for improvement and a place where Six Sigma is even more applicable to transactional processes than to manufacturing processes.

For years manufacturing processes have focused on scrap, rework, and cycle time because in manufacturing, failures pile up in the scrap bin and are visible. In transaction processes, failures tend to be hidden in people's in-boxes or "I'll get to it later" piles. In the case of healthcare claim processing, many systems are designed to handle rejected claims or a certain level of incorrectly paid claims. What if the system could be designed such that incorrect claims would never get into the system and all information needed to process the claim was present when it did arrive? In the context of this, we need to think of quality costs as any cost incurred when the process does not perform perfectly.

ROLLED THROUGHPUT YIELD

A key point in Six Sigma is the concept of rolled throughput yield. Rolled throughput yield has application in any process where the items are processed or transactions are subject to rework or reprocessing. For example, a purchase order is generated and during the approval process an error is detected. The purchase order has to go back to the originator for correction and then it reenters the process. This is an example of rework. Any time an item requires additional processing due to an error, unnecessary expense or delay is incurred. The idea behind rolled throughput yield is to highlight those areas where this waste occurs.

Let's look at a three-step process where each step has a 90% first-time yield, and all items eventually make it all the way through the process. We will put 100 transactions into this process. In the end all claims are taken care of; however, there is 10% rework at each step. The traditional yield would be calculated as 100 transactions in and 100 transactions completed for a yield of 100%. If we look at rolled throughput yield, we account for the number of transactions that had to be touched again. See Figure 5.1.

Rolled throughput yield = $0.90 \times 0.90 \times 0.90 = 0.729$ or 72%. In other words, only 72% of the transactions went through the process without additional work. The difference between the traditional yield of 100% and the rolled throughput yield is referred to as

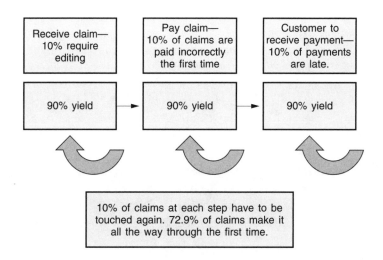

Figure 5.1 Example of rolled throughput yield in processing claims.

the *hidden factory* and highlights additional work required to complete transactions when there is some sort of process failure, which is also additional cost.

Rolled throughput yield (RTY) is often calculated using the Poisson distribution. RTY is the probability of a transaction going completely through the process without failure. The Poisson probability is given by:

$$p = \frac{e^{-\lambda} \lambda^{x}}{X!}, \lambda = \text{average number of events and } x = \text{occurrences.}$$

If the defects per unit (dpu), another way of saying average number of events, is substituted for the average number of events and we look for the probability of zero occurrences (zero defects), we have the probability that at a given defect per unit level a transaction will make it through the process with zero defects the first time.

Substitute 0.3 for dpu (90% yield at three process steps, 0.1 dpu per step) and zero for the number of occurrences (*x*) to calculate the probability of one item completing the process without rework.

$$p = \frac{e^{-dpu} dpu^{x}}{X!} = \frac{e^{-0.3} 0.3^{0}}{0!} = \frac{0.74(1)}{1} = 0.74$$

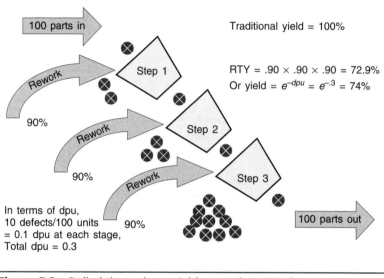

Traditional yield = 100%

RTY = .90 × .90 × .90 = 72.9%
Or yield = e^{-dpu} = $e^{-.3}$ = 74%

90%

90%

In terms of dpu,
10 defects/100 units
= 0.1 dpu at each stage,
Total dpu = 0.3

90%

Figure 5.2   Rolled throughput yield example using the bucket analogy.

Using this you see that it becomes a very good estimator for yield when data are recorded in defects per unit, 72% versus 74%.

You can also think in term of the process steps being buckets and a little is spilled between each bucket. See Figure 5.2. The spilled material is then collected and put back in the bucket at the point it fell out. Although all of the material that started the process will get into the final bucket, extra work is required to collect the material and put it back into the process.

LOSS FUNCTION

Genichi Taguchi, a Japanese engineer and quality pioneer, believed that as a product deviates from its target specification, the level of quality, customer satisfaction, decreases and cost increases. As mentioned in an earlier example, if a customer had the expectation that it takes 20 minutes to open a bank account, any deviation from that 20 minutes would result in a lesser quality experience for that customer. In the practical world we tend to put specifications on things, so we may say that the requirement for opening an account is 20

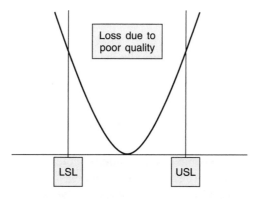

Figure 5.3 A Taguchi loss function diagram showing that the loss due to poor quality increases as the product or service approaches specification limits.

minutes ±5 minutes. As long as the time required to open the account is between the 15-minute lower specification limit (LSL) and the 25-minute upper specification limit (USL), we say we have met the goal. The point Taguchi was trying to make is that the chosen specification points have no real meaning. What makes 14 minutes that much worse than 15 minutes? And why is 14.9 minutes unacceptable, while 15.1 minutes would be considered acceptable? The explanation is that any time we are not at exactly 20 minutes, the customer is not completely satisfied, and the further we get from the 20 minutes the customer becomes increasingly dissatisfied and the loss due to poor quality increases. See Figure 5.3. This, of course, makes the Six Sigma point for centering the process and reducing variation.

MEASUREMENT SYSTEM EVALUATION

Arguably the most important and most overlooked element of any process improvement effort is the measuring system. We rely on the measuring system to provide data to make decisions. How often do we actually question the measuring system? This is an area where manufacturing Six Sigma far exceeds the capability of transactional Six Sigma, but it doesn't have to be that way.

In manufacturing, the measurement systems are constantly monitored and evaluated with calibrations systems and gage studies. On the transactional side, we have people making decisions at every step in the process based on their experience and judgment. Their decisions become critical inputs into the process. Those decisions could be how a customer is responded to or how much to pay against a given claim. In some cases there will be more variation due to the measurement system than to the process itself.

Let's consider the process of interviewing and hiring a candidate for a job. The candidate completes an application, the application is reviewed, and a determination is made whether or not to interview the candidate. If the very same application was given to three different managers, would they all make the same decision? They should, as there is no variation in the application. Any difference in decision is completely due to variation in the way the manager reviews and interprets the application.

Now consider the next step in the process; if those three managers interview the candidate, will they come to the same conclusion? In a good process the decision of all three should be the same, any variation will come from the interviewers as they are interviewing the same person and the person can either do the job or not.

What about when we evaluate employees? If two managers evaluate the same employee, will the results be the same? They should, as it is the same employee. One may argue that this variation is normal because different people see things in different ways. This argument is very true, but is this how we should make critical decisions in a transactional process? Where objective measurements are not possible, a subjective measurement system must be made repeatable to ensure accurate decisions.

There are two major ways to evaluate a measurement system and the choice is based solely on the type of data you collect. There is attribute gage repeatability and reproducibility (R&R) for attribute/discrete data and variable gage R&R for continuous measurement data.

Attribute Gage R&R

In situations where the measuring system yields attribute data, that is, pass/fail-type data where the transaction met the requirement or not, the measuring system can be evaluated using an attribute measuring system. In attribute measuring system analysis at least two evaluators and 30 samples are used where possible. Each sample will be evaluated twice by each evaluator and a determination made as to its acceptability. The expert's results or standard will also be recorded. Results can be recorded as in Table 5.2.

Table 5.2 Results of attribute gage study.

Sample	Evaluator 1		Evaluator 2		Expert
	Trial 1	Trial 2	Trial 1	Trial 2	
1	Accept	Accept	Accept	Accept	Accept
2	Accept	Accept	Accept	Accept	Accept
3	Accept	Accept	Accept	Accept	Accept
4	Accept	Accept	Accept	Accept	Accept
5	Accept	Accept	Accept	Accept	Accept
6	Accept	Accept	Accept	Accept	Accept
7	Accept	Accept	Accept	Accept	Accept
8	Accept	Accept	Accept	Accept	Accept
9	Accept	Accept	Accept	Accept	Accept
10	Accept	Accept	Accept	Accept	Accept
11	Accept	Accept	Accept	Accept	Accept
12	Accept	Accept	Accept	Accept	Accept
13	Accept	Accept	Accept	Accept	Accept
14	Accept	Accept	Accept	Accept	Reject
15	Reject	Reject	Reject	Reject	Reject
16	Reject	Reject	Reject	Reject	Reject
17	Reject	Reject	Reject	Reject	Reject
18	Reject	Reject	Reject	Reject	Reject
19	Reject	Reject	Reject	Reject	Reject
20	Reject	Reject	Reject	Reject	Reject
21	Reject	Reject	Reject	Reject	Reject
22	Reject	Reject	Accept	Reject	Reject
23	Reject	Accept	Reject	Reject	Reject
24	Reject	Reject	Reject	Reject	Reject
25	Reject	Reject	Reject	Accept	Reject
26	Accept	Accept	Accept	Accept	Accept
27	Accept	Accept	Accept	Accept	Accept
28	Reject	Accept	Accept	Reject	Accept
29	Accept	Reject	Accept	Accept	Accept
30	Accept	Accept	Accept	Accept	Accept

In the analysis of the measurement system, using the data in Table 5.2, three evaluations are performed:

1. *Within evaluator error.* Did the evaluators agree with themselves between each trial? Compare Trial 1 and Trial 2 columns for each evaluator. We see that Evaluator 1 disagreed with results between runs in samples 23, 28, and 29. This is a within agreement of 3 errors/30 trials = 10% disagreement or 90% agreement. Evaluator 2 disagreed with results between runs in samples 22, 25, and 28. This is a within agreement of 3 errors/30 trials = 10% disagreement or 90% agreement.

2. *Between evaluator error.* Did evaluators agree with each other? Compare Trial 1 and Trial 2 across all evaluators. Here, we see that Evaluators 1 and 2 disagreed on samples 22, 23, 25, 28, and 29 for a within agreement of 5/30 trials = 16% disagreement or 84% agreement.

3. *Agreement with expert.* Did evaluators agree with the expert or standard? Compare Trial 1 and Trial 2 across all evaluators and compare to expert column. Evaluator 1 disagreed with the standard or expert in trials 23 and 28. This is an evaluator versus standard agreement of 28/30 = 93%. Evaluator 2 disagreed with the standard or expert in trials 14, 22, 25, and 28. This is an evaluator versus standard agreement of 26/30 = 87%. Both evaluators agreed with themselves, each other, and the standard in 24 of the 30 trials for an overall agreement of 80%. The analysis can also be performed without the expert but only comparisons between the evaluators can be made. With this analysis we can say that the measurement system is 80% effective or the correct decision is made 80% of the time.

In most cases, attribute decision systems can be improved by training and developing standards to use when making decisions. The application of an attribute gage R&R should not be limited to analyzing decisions at measurement points. Consider any step in a process where a decision has to be made based on subjective inputs. If a customer calls with a complaint, will all customer service agents handle the complaint in the same manner? Will credits or returns be classified and handled the same by all agents at various locations? Do all salespeople make the same decision given similar circumstances? If the answer to any one of these questions is no, then there is an application for an attribute gage R&R. A more appropriate name for this tool would be an attribute decision analysis.

The challenge in such a study will be to collect the proper samples for the study. You will need several examples of transactions that are typical to the process. Some examples should be easy to classify either as acceptable or clearly not acceptable, while others should be in the gray area between what is acceptable or not. For example, if we are reviewing applications for job candidates, there should be several that are clearly qualified, several that are not qualified, and a few borderline applications. With a little thought, this type of analysis can be a simple and effective tool for evaluating and improving your decision system.

It helps to think of any decision point in a process as an inspection or evaluation point. Also any point in a process where a transaction would require an approval is really a form of inspection. The goal of the attribute gage R&R is to ensure that all evaluators, adjusters, or approval systems will make the same decision given the same set of circumstances.

Table 5.3 gives examples of various process decision points and their decisions that must be made through evaluation. Figure 5.4 gives

Table 5.3   Examples of various processes and the corresponding evaluation decisions.

Process	Decision to Evaluate
Production planning process	Difference in material ordered for a given project
Customer returns process	Difference in credits issued
Sales	Response to customer's questions
Customer service	Level of service a class of customer receives
Loan application	Approval differences between processors
Claims adjustments	Difference in adjustment amounts between adjustors
Loan or PO approval	Evaluation criteria used by different individuals
Job candidate interviewing	Hire decision
Resume screening	Decision to interview candidate

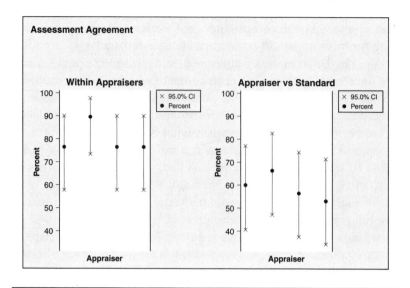

Figure 5.4   Attribute agreement analysis (attribute gage study) output from MINITAB.

an example MINITAB graph for an attribute agreement analysis. It shows the within appraiser agreement to be in the 75–90% range while the appraiser versus standard agreement is in the 50–70% range. This would indicate that the appraisers are reasonably consistent in their decision when evaluating the same transaction (within), however, they are only making the correct decision 50–70% of the time (appraiser versus standard).

Variable Gage R&R

On the surface, a variable gage R&R would seem to be a tool for exclusive use on manufacturing-type projects; however, if you consider the output of a transactional process as a variable, the tool becomes very useful. Take an example of paying medical claims by an insurance provider. If a claim is received, will all processors classify and pay the same amount for a particular claim?

The normal method of teaching variable gage R&R is to have two or more inspectors measure 10 parts for a particular dimension and then repeat the measurement. This would be a typical manufacturing Six Sigma example. Let's set up an experiment with 10 sample insurance claims and two claims processors. Using the claims as the parts and the processors as the inspectors, we could evaluate the dollars paid as the measurement variable. The results of this study would indicate how consistently the claims processors paid similar claims.

Variable gage R&R is really a specialized ANOVA used to identify key components of variation in a measuring system. I do not intend to show the details of the calculations in this text, as many sources are available for this, including the Automotive Industry Action Group and many software packages, but we will address the types of variation identified by the variable gage R&R.

When a variable gage R&R is performed, we wish to determine the variation of the measuring system under normal operating conditions. It is important to realize that measurement system variation can not be separated from process variation, that is, the measured process variation will include both variation from the process and variation from the measuring system. It always amazes me to see the number of Six Sigma projects that end up improving the measurement system to reach the target improvement levels.

In measurement systems we tend to think of the measurement as perfect when, in fact, that may not be the case. The example I use to illustrate this is the thermometer on the bank. Just because it says that it is 80 degrees outside doesn't mean that it really is 80 degrees! I am not sure of the source of this, but it has been said that a person with one watch always knows what time it is and a person with two watches never knows the time. This saying emphasizes both the trust we have in our measuring systems and the variation in those same measuring systems that we tend to take for granted.

Measures of measurement system variation include:

1. *Repeatability.* This is the ability of a measuring device in the measuring system to obtain the same measurement time after time.

2. *Reproducibility.* This is the ability of the person using the measuring device to obtain the same measurement time after time. Excess repeatability error would be due to the measuring device, not the person using it.

3. *Interaction.* This is the influence the combination of person and device have over the measuring system variation.

4. *Number of categories.* This is the number of distinct "bins" or categories the measured items can be classified into.

5. *Total gage R&R.* This is the sum of all variation in a measurement system.

6. *Part variation.* This is the amount of variation contributed by the items being measured.

According to most sources, a measurement system is acceptable if the total gage R&R is less than 30% of the tolerance, although it is desired to be 10% or less. The calculated number of categories should be four to five and more is better. A good measurement system will exhibit most all of its variation in part variation and very little in either repeatability or reproducibility. Note: Crossed gage studies are used when objects are not damaged by measurement and nested studies are used in destructive testing, where the same samples can not be retested.

Now, let's consider our insurance claims example. Figure 5.5 shows a MINITAB output for a simulated claims adjustment process where two claims adjustment specialists were compared using five sample claims.

The p-value can be used to determine the significance of either the adjuster's claim or the interaction of the two. (See discussion of the ANOVA p-value in Chapter 6.) In this case, looking at the two-way ANOVA table with interaction in Figure 5.5, the claim is significant (p-value less than 0.05), but the interaction of claim number and adjuster is not. This is what you want to see in a gage study as the items being evaluated should be more significant than the evaluation method.

The component of variation chart in Figure 5.6 indicates the percentage of variation in the study. You want to see at least 90% of the variation in part to part and very little in either reproducibility or repeatability. The range chart indicates the range between the adjuster's first and second evaluation of the same claim. The x-bar chart is the average of the adjusters' evaluation of the same claim. Here you expect most of the points to be outside the control limits

Gage R&R Study - ANOVA Method

Two-Way ANOVA Table With Interaction

```
Source                          DF       SS       MS        F       P
Claim Number                     4  1121070   280268  50.6584   0.001
Adjustment S                     1     3001     3001   0.5425   0.502
Claim Number * Adjustment S      4    22130     5533   1.4651   0.284
Repeatability                   10    37763     3776
Total                           19  1183964
```

Two-Way ANOVA Table Without Interaction

```
Source          DF       SS       MS        F       P
Claim Number     4  1121070   280268  65.5131   0.000
Adjustment S     1     3001     3001   0.7015   0.416
Repeatability   14    59893     4278
Total           19  1183964
```

Gage R&R

```
                             %Contribution
Source           VarComp     (of VarComp)
Total Gage R&R    4278.0             5.84
  Repeatability   4278.0             5.84
  Reproducibility    0.0             0.00
    Adjustment S     0.0             0.00
Part-To-Part     68997.4            94.16
Total Variation  73275.4           100.00


                                Study Var   %Study Var
Source           StdDev (SD)    (6 * SD)      (%SV)
Total Gage R&R        65.407       392.44      24.16
  Repeatability       65.407       392.44      24.16
  Reproducibility      0.000         0.00       0.00
    Adjustment S       0.000         0.00       0.00
Part-To-Part         262.673      1576.04      97.04
Total Variation      270.694      1624.17     100.00


Number of Distinct Categories = 5
```

Figure 5.5 MINITAB gage R&R interpretation.

because the parts should have more variation than the measuring system. The adjustment amount by claim number chart is the average of all adjusters for each claim. The difference between claims is not important, but you expect to see very little variation of any given claim. The adjustment amount by adjustment specialist is the average of all claims by specialist. In this case, the spread is not important, but the average for each adjuster should be the same in a good

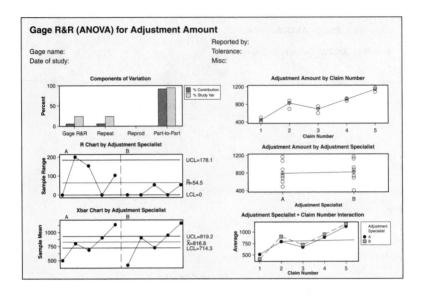

Figure 5.6 Variable gage R&R output from MINITAB using adjustment dollars as the variable.

Table 5.4 Processes and potential process measures.

Process	Measurement system to evaluate
Claims adjustments	Adjustment dollars
Job candidate interviewing	Interview score
Performance reviews	Scoring by different managers

evaluation system. The final chart in Figure 5.6 shows the interaction between claim and adjuster. If the lines on any given segment are not parallel, this would indicate there is interaction between the claim and adjuster, and for some reason different claims are handled differently by different adjusters.

Table 5.4 lists sample processes with examples of the measuring system to be evaluated. The process measure to be evaluated will evolve from the key process measure used to track the project.

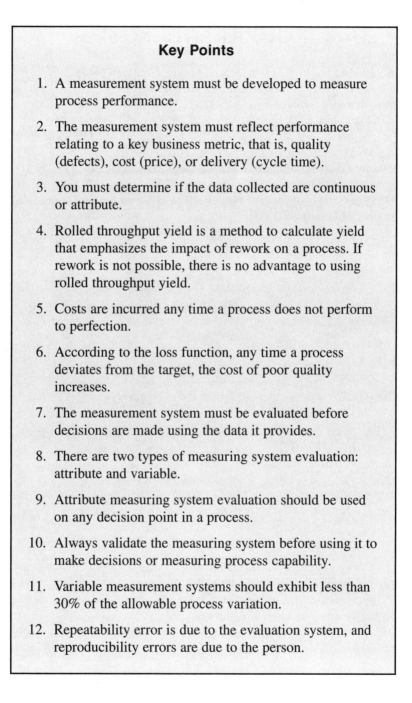

Key Points

1. A measurement system must be developed to measure process performance.

2. The measurement system must reflect performance relating to a key business metric, that is, quality (defects), cost (price), or delivery (cycle time).

3. You must determine if the data collected are continuous or attribute.

4. Rolled throughput yield is a method to calculate yield that emphasizes the impact of rework on a process. If rework is not possible, there is no advantage to using rolled throughput yield.

5. Costs are incurred any time a process does not perform to perfection.

6. According to the loss function, any time a process deviates from the target, the cost of poor quality increases.

7. The measurement system must be evaluated before decisions are made using the data it provides.

8. There are two types of measuring system evaluation: attribute and variable.

9. Attribute measuring system evaluation should be used on any decision point in a process.

10. Always validate the measuring system before using it to make decisions or measuring process capability.

11. Variable measurement systems should exhibit less than 30% of the allowable process variation.

12. Repeatability error is due to the evaluation system, and reproducibility errors are due to the person.

CHAPTER REFERENCES

Automotive Industry Action Group (AIAG). *Measurement System Analysis.* 3rd ed. Southfield, MI: AIAG, 2002.

http://www.isixsigma.com.

Kiemele, Mark J., Stephen R. Schmidt, and Ronald J. Berbine. *Basic Statistics, Tools for Continuous Improvement.* 4th ed. Colorado Springs, CO: Air Academy Press, 2000.

Quality Council of Indiana. *CSSBB Primer.* Terre Haute, IN: Quality Council of Indiana, 2001.

Windsor, Samuel. "Attribute Gage R&R," *Six Sigma Forum Magazine* 2, no. 4 (August 2003): 23–28.

6

Measuring Process Capability

PROCESS CAPABILITY MEASURES

Once we have determined the key process performance measures and validated the measuring system, we are ready to compare the performance of the process to the customer specification. This comparison must be performed to determine the percentage of time the process will produce an acceptable output. Process capability is a baseline measurement to determine how well the customer requirements are being met.

In any process capability study two items are required: a measure of process variation and the specifications of the process. Process capability is simply the ratio between the two. The one we choose is dependent on the type of data we collect from the process. We will concern ourselves with three basic data types, which will describe the majority of projects that Green Belts will encounter. All of the data types could be converted in a standard measure called process sigma, if desired. In early stages of Six Sigma deployment, it is important to choose a capability measure that those involved understand. In this section we will present different measures or indexes to use. Typically you would only use one type of capability to measure a particular process output. See Table 6.1 for a summary of data types.

Table 6.1 Summary of data types.

Data Type	Units
Continuous	Dollars, time
Attribute	Pass/fail Accept/reject
Discrete	Errors per page Complaints per week

Continuous Data

Measurement data are considered continuous data or variable data. That is because the data depend on how they are measured. For example, if we were to measure cycle time with a clock that only read in minutes, one minute would be the finest graduation we could report. If we made that same measurement in seconds, we could report seconds. We could continue to measure in finer and finer increments as long as a measuring tool with enough precision was available, thus the data are considered continuous.

In transactional projects we can consider time and dollars as continuous data. Determining the process capability in continuous data consists in comparing the variation and average of the data to some specification to determine the degree to which the requirement is met. Continuous process capabilities are typically reported in terms of *Cp* or *Cpk*. The use of *Cp* and *Cpk* assumes the data are normally distributed. In the event the data are not normally distributed, more advanced tools can be applied to calculate *Cp* and *Cpk*.

$$Cp = \frac{USL - LSL}{6\sigma} \qquad Cpk = \frac{X - LSL}{3\sigma}, \frac{USL - X}{3\sigma}$$

where USL = upper specification limit, LSL = lower specification limit, X = process average, and σ = process standard deviation.

Cp is a ratio of the tolerance USL–LSL to the process spread (6σ) six times the process standard deviation. A *Cp* of 1.0 means that 100% of the tolerance is used by the process; a *Cp* of 2.0 means that only 50% of the tolerance is used.

Cpk is used when process centering is a factor. *Cpk* is calculated from both the upper and lower specification limits. The lower of the two values is reported as the process *Cpk*. When continuous data are available, the data can be directly converted into a process sigma value instead of reporting a *Cp* or *Cpk* value.

Let's consider our drive to work example. Our drive to work takes 20 minutes on average with a standard deviation of two minutes. We wish to leave home at 7:35 AM. What is the *Cp* and *Cpk?*

First we must determine the specification limits. We know we need to be at work between 7:45 and 8:00. The lower specification limit would be 10 minutes (7:45–7:35) and the upper specification would be 25 minutes (8:00–7:35). So, in order to be at work between 7:45 and 8:00 while leaving home at 7:35, we will meet our goal if the ride takes anywhere between 10 and 25 minutes.

$$Cp = \frac{USL - LSL}{6\sigma}$$

$$Cp = \frac{25 - 10}{6 \times 2} = 1.25$$

The *Cp* of our process = 1.25. A *Cp* greater than one means that the process uses less than 100% of the available tolerance. This indicates we are capable of arriving at work on time. *Cp* only considers variation and not the centering of the process, as there is no provision for specification limits in the equation.

Cpk addresses the issues of process centering by including the specification limits in the equation. To calculate *Cpk* you must do both the upper and lower calculation and report the lesser of the two.

$$Cpk = \frac{X - LSL}{3\sigma}, \frac{USL - X}{3\sigma}$$

$$Cpk \text{ lower, } Cpk = \frac{20 - 10}{3 \times 2} = 1.67$$

$$Cpk \text{ upper, } Cpk = \frac{25 - 20}{3 \times 2} = 0.83$$

Since we only report the lesser of the two, our process *Cpk* is 0.83. A *Cpk* of less than 1.33 is considered not capable of meeting requirements. This indicates that if we leave home at 7:35, as we wish, we will not consistently meet the requirement of arriving at work between 7:45 and 8:00.

If the process average had been 17.5 instead of 20, both the *Cp* and *Cpk* would have been 1.25. It is useful to think of the *Cp* as the best it can be and the *Cpk* of what it actually is. In this case, process variation and centering must be improved to make the process capable. Using the *Z* transform (that will be discussed later), we can determine the exact percentage of time we will be late for work using this process. Data in this section are assumed to be normally distributed; nonnormal data will be addressed in a later chapter.

In another example of process capability, process time data were collected for 125 transactions over a period of one week. The average time to process an application was 100 minutes with a standard deviation of 20 minutes. The time required to process the applications is between 60 and 140 minutes. What is the *Cp* and *Cpk?*

We can solve this using the formula just stated or we could use MINITAB by entering each data point and using the process capability tool. See Appendix B for the required key strokes. Figure 6.1 shows the MINITAB output.

Attribute Data

When an output has only certain outcomes, like pass or fail, acceptable or not acceptable, it is considered attribute data. If we count the total number of customers serviced in a given period of time and determined what percentage of customers was satisfied, this would be a measure of attribute process capability. When only two outcomes are possible, this is called binominal capability. Binominal process capabilities are normally reported in average percentages. The average defect rate is then compared to the customer's requirement to determine if the process is capable.

$$p = \frac{\sum defects}{\sum units}$$

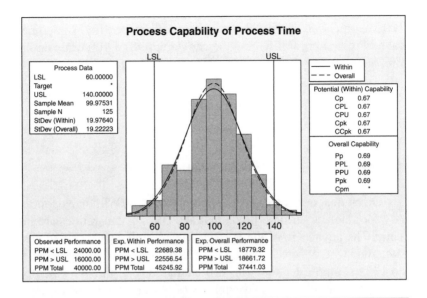

Figure 6.1   Process capability for process time.

For example, if in 100 trips to work we are late one time, we can say our binominal process capability is 1% defective or 99% acceptable.

Discrete Data

Discrete data are any data that we count. We could count the number of errors per report that are generated over a period of time. The average errors per report would be considered discrete data process capability. The average defects per unit is then compared to the customer's requirement to determine if the process is capable. Discrete data are modeled using the Poisson distribution.

$$\text{Average defects per units} = \frac{\sum defects}{\sum units}$$

Consider our drive to work example. If we were to determine the capability of the number of times the car started on the first try in

100 attempts, we could use discrete process capability, sometimes called Poisson capability. Say the car started 98 of 100 trials on the first attempt.

$$AvgDPU = \frac{\sum defects}{\sum units}$$

$$AvgDPU = \frac{2}{100} = 0.02$$

Given this, our Poisson capability is 0.02 dpu. With one opportunity for a defect per unit, binominal and Poisson capabilities are the same. The advantage of the Poisson capability is that it can address situations where there is more than one opportunity for a defect per unit. For example, let's say we verified that the car started on the first try and we had more than five gallons of gas in the car. The example could then become, the car started on 98 of the 100 attempts and on three occasions we had less than the required five gallons of gas. The total number of defects would then be five and the number of units would remain the same for a Poisson capability of 0.05 defects per unit. To convert this into a percent acceptable, you would need to use the equation e^{-dpu}, where e is the exponential approximately equal to 2.718. In this case, the percent acceptable would be $e^{-0.05}$ or 0.95 (95%). This will be useful if you wish to convert a Poisson capability into a measure of process sigma, as we will discuss later.

Reporting Process Capability

There are many ways to report process capability. The calculation can be made and the data left in their original form (*Cpk*, average percent rejection, average defects per unit) or they could be converted into a standard measure such as a sigma value. There are advantages and disadvantages to each. If the capability measure is left in its original format, *Cpk*, for example, it may be easy to understand and communicate for those used to working with it, as long as all processes can be measured using *Cpk*.

Converting various measures into a sigma value is useful when comparing unlike processes, such as comparing a continuous data process to an attribute data process. The disadvantage is that most Green Belt candidates do not have a feel for how the sigma value relates to the percent defective or percent acceptable. See Figure 6.2 for a comparison of sigma values to percent acceptable.

Before we describe sigma values, we should cover the Z transform. At this point it is important to understand the concept and not worry too much about the actual math. The Z transform tells us the percentage of area under the curve for a normal distribution beyond a certain value. This is important in understanding process capability because if we use the specification as the value we are interested in, we have a direct method for determining the percentage that does not meet the requirement. The Z value just happens to be the sigma value of our process.

For example, we know that our drive to work takes an average of 20 minutes and the data indicate the standard deviation is two minutes. From this and the Z transform, we can determine the percentage of time that it will take less than 25 minutes to get to work. (A continuous data example without calculating *Cp* or *Cpk*.)

First we calculate the Z value, as follows:

$$Z = \frac{X - \mu}{\sigma}$$

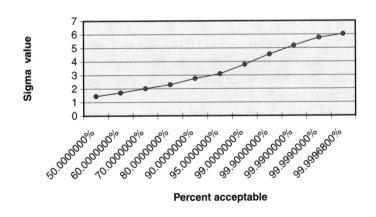

Figure 6.2 Process sigma versus percent acceptable.

Our Z becomes, $(25 - 20)/2 = 2.5$, where X is the value of interest, μ (the average) is 20, and σ (standard deviation) is 2. With the Z value, we look in a table for the cumulative normal distribution under a Z value of 2.5, and we see that the area under the curve up to 25 is 0.9938. See a sample of a section of a Z table in Table 6.2. (Z tables can be found in most any quality or statistics book).

If you do not have a table, the Z value can be found in Microsoft Excel using the NORMDIST function and entering the Z value. Values can be calculated in MINITAB using calc, probability distribution normal using a mean of zero, and a standard deviation of one. Use "inverse cumulative probability" to go from a percentage to a Z value and "cumulative probability" to go from a Z value to a percentage.

All this tells us that 99.38% of the time our drive to work will take less than 25 minutes. With this information, we know that if we leave for work at 7:35 AM, we will be late 0.62% (1–0.9938) of the time.

So what does the Z value have to do with the sigma of the process? The fact is that the Z value is the sigma of the process with a twist. That twist is probably the most confusing part of Six Sigma and why six sigma is really not six sigma at all.

In Six Sigma we say that the average of the process will move around over time. For example, our drive to work, on average, may take a little longer in the winter than in the summer. The problem is that we really do not know what the difference in average drive time is. So we need a way to predict what variation of the average will be. To do this we use a standard value of 1.5 sigma. So we say the average over time will move around by about 1.5 standard deviations. In our example, the standard deviation is 2. With this we would estimate that, over time, the process average would vary by about 1.5 × two or three minutes.

While it is interesting to know how much the average moves over time, we really need to understand how the defect rate is

Table 6.2 Sample data from Z table.

Z	0.09	0.08	0.07	0.06	0.05	0.04	0.03	0.02	0.01	0.00
2.5	0.9952	0.9951	0.9949	0.9948	0.9946	0.9945	0.9943	0.9941	0.9940	0.9938

affected by this *shift and drift,* as it is called. By calculating the short-term process sigma and subtracting 1.5 from that number, we have a reasonable estimate of long-term process performance. The short-term sigma will always be higher (better) than the long-term sigma due to the drift over time. The value of 1.5 sigma comes from the early work of Mikel Harry, who determined that most processes, on average, drift by this amount. We will use this value unless we have data to support another value.

In our example, we could say we have a short-term process sigma of 2.5 or a long-term process sigma of one. (2.5 − 1.5 = 1). So why is a Six Sigma process not always six sigma? It is because a process that is said to be six sigma in the short term is really a 4.5 sigma process in the long term. If you calculate the area under the curve for six standard deviations, as we will do in a moment, you will find that it equals about one defect in one billion, and not 3.4 defects per million (the value associated with six sigma). If, however, you were to do the same calculation with 4.5 standard deviations, you would find that it equals about 3.4 defects per million, thus building in the 1.5 sigma shift.

So how does this help us? As mentioned earlier, unlike processes can be measured on the sigma scale. To do this you need to convert your process measure into a percent defective, use the Z transform in reverse to get the Z value, and then add or subtract 1.5 depending on if the data collected are long- or short-term.

Instead of looking at the time it takes us to drive to work, let's consider that over the last 100 days we were late one time, a binominal example. What is our process sigma? We know we were late 1% of the time. We look at the table of Z values in Table 6.3 and find the nearest value to 0.99. It happens to be 0.9901 and the Z value is 2.33. In Excel the NORMSINV function can be used; just enter the percent defective. This means we have a long-term sigma of 2.33, if we consider 100 days to be long-term.

Table 6.3 Using Z table to determine Z value when given a percentage.

	0.09	0.08	0.07	0.06	0.05	0.04	0.03	0.02	0.01	0.00
2.3	0.9916	0.9913	0.9911	0.9909	0.9906	0.9904	0.9901	0.9898	0.9896	0.9893

When reporting sigma values, there is confusion over whether the data are long-term or short-term. The one you choose really depends on your process and how the data are collected. It really doesn't matter if long-term or short-term sigma values are reported, as long as everyone understands which they are and the same value is used consistently. Typically binominal and Poisson data are considered long-term in their collected form, while continuous data are considered short-term.

Poisson data can also be converted into a sigma value. Using the dpu of 0.05 from the earlier example, we said that the percent acceptable was 95%. Using the Z table or Excel we find that 95% is equal to a Z of 1.64 or a long-term process sigma of 1.64.

Typically when a process is said to be six sigma, it means that it is a sigma process in the short-term and a 4.5 sigma long-term process. You can easily see this by looking up 4.5 in a Z table or using the NORMDIST function in Excel. For a Z of 4.5 you get 0.9999966 or 99.99966% acceptable, which gives us the magic six sigma number 3.4 defects per million. $1,000,000 - (1,000,000 \times 0.9999966) = 3.4$. So you see a Six Sigma process is actually 4.5 sigma in the long term. See Figure 6.3 comparing long- and short-term sigma values to percent acceptable.

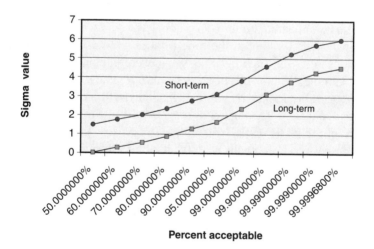

Figure 6.3 Sigma value versus percent acceptable comparing long- and short-term data.

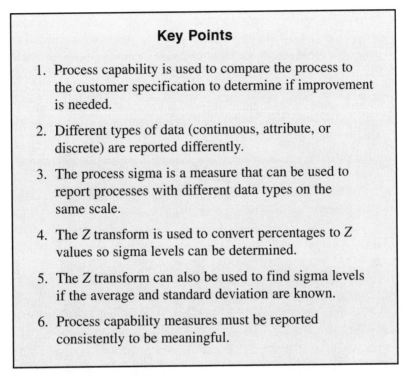

Key Points

1. Process capability is used to compare the process to the customer specification to determine if improvement is needed.

2. Different types of data (continuous, attribute, or discrete) are reported differently.

3. The process sigma is a measure that can be used to report processes with different data types on the same scale.

4. The Z transform is used to convert percentages to Z values so sigma levels can be determined.

5. The Z transform can also be used to find sigma levels if the average and standard deviation are known.

6. Process capability measures must be reported consistently to be meaningful.

CHAPTER REFERENCES

Automotive Industry Action Group (AIAG). *Advanced Product Quality Planning and Control Plan* (June 1994).

Boeing. *Advanced Quality System Tools, D1-9000-1* (November 1998).

Juran, Joseph M., and A. Blanton Godfrey. *Juran's Quality Handbook.* 5th ed. New York: McGraw-Hill, 1999.

Quality Council of Indiana. *CSSBB Primer.* Terre Haute, IN: Quality Council of Indiana, 2001.

7

Relating Inputs to Outputs

At this point in the project, we have:

1. Gained an understanding of the process through process mapping.

2. Identified the process inputs and outputs on the process map.

3. Determined what can go wrong with the process inputs that will affect the outputs using FMEA.

4. Determined a key process measure based on the output of the process.

5. Compared the process measure to the specification or customer requirement using some type of capability measure.

6. Using the process capability measures, determined the gap between current process performance and desired process performance.

If the process is capable of consistently meeting the required performance at high sigma levels, there is no need to proceed. Most likely this is not the case. In this chapter we will further investigate the relationships of the process inputs to the process outputs, with the goal of defining and quantifying those relationships. Another way of thinking about this is that we are trying to determine what makes a difference in our process. For example, if we were to measure customer satisfaction, does the amount of time the customer had to wait for service impact the level of satisfaction? Or we may ask if there is a difference in the sales volume between two sales locations or if the average cycle time for loan processing is shorter at one bank than another. Determining whether or not this relationship or difference exists is called *hypothesis testing.*

To do hypothesis testing, several additional tools will be added to the toolbox. The selection of the correct tool will be dependent on the question we are attempting to answer and the type of data we have. We will classify the inputs and outputs as continuous and attribute. When an input is classified as continuous, that means we can measure the output. Dollars, satisfaction measures, and time would be considered continuous inputs or outputs. Attribute inputs or outputs can be thought of as groupings. If we know the types of service performed and whether the customer was satisfied or not, we would have both an attribute input and attribute output. Type of service would be a group and satisfied versus not satisfied would be another group or category.

HYPOTHESIS TESTS

It is important to understand the role of hypothesis testing in Six Sigma. When hypothesis tests are performed, we are attempting to not only determine if the input variable is related to the output variable, but whether the relationship is statistically significant. That means, is the relationship real or is it due to random variation? These tests are typically performed at a 95% confidence level (alpha risk of 0.05). To perform the test, we establish what is called the null hypothesis and the alternate hypothesis. Think of the null hypothesis as "no relationship exists" and the alternate hypothesis as "a relationship does exist."

In a hypothesis test we set the null and alternate hypotheses, perform a statistical test, and, from that test, determine if we are going to accept or reject the null hypothesis. If we accept the null hypothesis, we say that no relationship exists. If we reject the null hypothesis, we say the input variable is related to or has an effect on the output variable. Statistically this is an area in which Six Sigma tends to bend the rules a little, as the null hypothesis is never actually accepted. It is like a jury saying you are not guilty, but never really saying you are innocent. In true statistical terms the null hypothesis can only be rejected or not rejected. In practical terms, as far as Six Sigma projects go, we do accept or reject the null hypothesis. This will no doubt upset some of my statistical friends but remember, in Six Sigma we are training problem solvers not statisticians.

Without a doubt, hypothesis testing is the most confusing part of Six Sigma training, but by remembering a few key items this confusion can be removed. It is important to keep in mind the difference between statistical significance and practical significance. In many cases, you may find that an input may not have a significant relationship to the output, but it is easy to control and will not hurt anything if it is controlled, so why not control it?

Write the Null Hypothesis

When doing a hypothesis test, always write the null and alternate hypotheses. This advice is like advice from your parents. They tell you over and over, but you never do it, and you find out later that they were right! So many times students try to answer a question without writing the question down, and this will lead to confusion when trying to relate the statistical answer back to the practical answer. In hypothesis testing you must define the problem in practical terms, convert the question into a statistical question, collect data, perform a statistical test, determine the result of the statistical test, and, finally, convert the results of that test back into a practical answer.

Let's consider these steps:

1. *Define the practical problem.* Say, for example, you want to determine if there is a difference between the sales volume at two locations. We would set the null hypothesis as there is no difference in the sales at the two locations.

Sales location A has the same sales volume as location B.

Sales location A does not have the same sales volume as location B.

2. *Convert to a statistical problem.* Written statistically this problem would be:

H_0: Sales at A = Sales at B.

In this case, the alternate hypothesis would be that there is a difference between the sales at location A and location B, written as:

H_a: Sales at A ≠ Sales at B.

3. *Collect data.* In this case, we would take sample data from each of the two locations, perform a two-sample *t*-test, and determine if we are going to accept or reject the null hypothesis. In this step, before trying to say one is different from the other, go back to the null and alternate hypotheses you have written down. Do you accept or reject the null hypothesis? If the *p*-value is greater than 0.05, we accept, and if the *p*-value is less than 0.05, we reject the null hypothesis.

4. *Convert the results of the statistical test back to the practical problem.* If the null hypothesis is accepted, we choose:

H_0: Sales at location A are equal to or no different from sales at location B.

If we reject the null hypothesis, we choose

H_a: Sales at location A are different from sales at location B.

Which answers the original question? Until you get some experience with hypothesis testing, going though this process will eliminate confusion.

Alpha and Beta Risks

To further confuse things, students are introduced to the concept of alpha and beta risks. It is important to understand that any time we perform a statistical test there are four possible outcomes. Think in terms of the earlier sales example and remember that, in reality, the sales are either the same at the two locations or they are not the same. The problem is that we really do not know which is true, so we perform a test to determine this.

Another example would be when you go to the doctor to get checked for a certain disease; in reality, you either have the disease or you don't. The doctor, however, does not know the true state, so the doctor performs a test. The test, however, may not be 100% accurate and it may say you have the disease when you don't or may say you do not have the disease when, in fact, you do.

In hypothesis testing there are two ways to make the correct decision and two ways to make the incorrect decision. This is where the alpha and beta risks apply. See Table 7.1.

H_0: You do not have the disease.

H_a: You have the disease

The alpha risk is the risk of rejecting the null hypothesis when it is true. This risk is typically set at 5%. This means that there is a 5% risk that the doctor will say you have the disease when in fact you do not have the disease.

The beta risk is the risk of accepting that the alternate hypothesis (not rejecting the null) is true. In our medical example, it's the risk that the doctor will say you do not have the disease when, in fact, you do have the disease. This risk is typically set at 10% for most Six Sigma applications.

The confidence level (1 – alpha risk) of the test, usually set at 95% (5% alpha risk) is the probability that the doctor will say you do not have the disease when you actually do not have it, a correct decision.

Table 7.1 Description of alpha and beta risks.

True State	Test Results Indicate	
	Do not have the disease	Have the disease
Do not have the disease	(1 – alpha) Probability of accepting null when it is true (correct decision)	Alpha risk probability of rejecting the null when it is true (Type 1 error)
Have the disease	Beta probability of accepting the null when it is false (Type II error)	Power (1 – beta) probability of rejecting the null when it is false (correct decision)

Table 7.2 Tool selection table based on type of inputs and outputs.

	Input	
Output	**Continuous**	**Categorical**
Continuous	Regression	*t*-test, ANOVA
Categorical	Logistic regression	Chi-square table

The power of the test (1 – beta risk) is the probability that if you have the disease the doctor will say that you have the disease. It's a correct decision.

Once the concept of hypothesis testing is understood, it is just a matter of choosing the correct test to apply. That choice is based on the type of data you are dealing with. Thinking in terms of the toolbox, if you have a nail to drive, you would select a hammer. If you have to install a screw, you would choose a screwdriver. See Table 7.2.

Hypothesis testing tool selection is really no different. Tool selection depends on the data type of the input and output. For example if you have categorical inputs like *supplier,* and you wanted to determine if there is a difference in cycle time, a continuous output, you see from Table 7.2 that ANOVA is the correct tool.

The *p*-Value

Today, software packages make hypothesis testing fairly straightforward. You enter the data, perform the proper test, and the software returns the results with a *p*-value. At the 95% confidence level, if the *p*-value is less than 0.05, you reject the null hypothesis. If the *p*-value is greater than 0.05, you cannot reject the null hypothesis, and, in Six Sigma, we say there is no difference or no relationship. The *p*-value is defined as the probability that you would get a value more extreme than the observed value if the null hypothesis were true.

If software is not available, all of the hypothesis tests can be performed manually. When tests are done manually, you typically compare a tabulated value, based on degrees of freedom from a statistical table, to a calculated value. If the calculated value is greater than the tabulated value, you reject the null hypothesis, and if the calculated value is less than the tabulated value, you fail to reject or accept the null hypothesis. The *p*-value can be found by determining the area under the curve beyond the calculated value of the appropriate test. Details of performing these tests can be found in most statistics books.

ONE-TAILED VERSUS TWO-TAILED TESTS

In hypothesis testing it is necessary to determine whether you want to perform a one-tailed or two-tailed hypothesis test. This decision must be made when using either the *t* distribution, *F* distribution, or chi-square distribution. When doing a hypothesis test, we are trying to determine if one sample is significantly different from another or if a sample is significantly different from a historic mean.

The two-tailed test is used when we are interested because the difference is either higher or lower. For example, say we were looking at call volumes during a particular time of the day for staffing purposes, and we knew that five customer service representatives were required to handle 50 calls an hour. We could look at average call volumes at different times of the day and compare them to the 50 calls per hour that the system is capable of handling. We would be interested if the call volume was either significantly higher or lower than the 50 calls per hour. If it was higher, we would need to add people, and if it was lower, we could use those people for other things. In this case, the test would be a two-tailed test because we would reject the null hypothesis if the volume was either above or below the test mean of 50.

On the other hand, we may only be interested if the call volume is significantly above 50 calls per hour. We would then use a one-tailed test. The one-tailed test only rejects the null if the call rate is above the 50 per hour level. It is possible to use the one-tailed test for a two-tailed application; however, the alpha risk changes by half. If a two-tailed test (see Figure 7.1) has an alpha risk of 0.05, it actually means that there is an alpha risk of 0.025 on each side of the distribution. The same alpha risk applied to a one-tailed test would have the entire 0.05 risk in one tail of the distribution (see Figure 7.2).

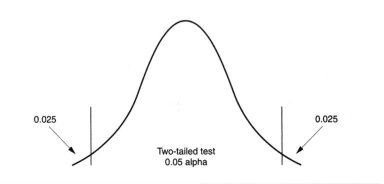

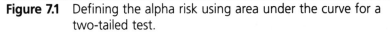

Figure 7.1 Defining the alpha risk using area under the curve for a two-tailed test.

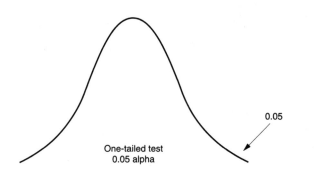

Figure 7.2 Defining the alpha risk using area under the curve for a one-tailed test.

ATTRIBUTE INPUT AND CONTINUOUS OUTPUT

The most common combination of input and output is an attribute input and continuous output. Consider an example where we want to investigate whether the region of the country has an impact on claims processed. The input would be "region" (a grouping or category) and the output would be measurable in terms of sales dollars, which is continuous.

The three most common hypothesis tests a Green Belt will use in a situation involving an attribute input and continuous outputs are:

1. One-sample *t*-test

2. Two-sample *t*-test

3. Analysis of variance (ANOVA)

Once again, the selection is based on the data and the question you are attempting to answer. Back to the toolbox with a categorical input and continuous output, we determine we need one of those three tools. See Table 7.3. Which particular tool is dependent on the data available, as follows:

1. If you are comparing a recently collected sample of data to that of a historic or known mean, you would select the one-sample *t*-test. If, for example, it is known from historic data that the sales volume is \$5000 per day, you make a change to the process and wish to determine if the change made a difference. You could compare the sales volume from a sample of days selected since the change and perform a one-sample *t*-test to determine if there is, in fact, a difference between the sales volume before and after the change.

2. If you wanted to compare the sales volume between two locations, you could select a sample from each location, perform a two-sample *t*-test, and determine if there is a difference between the two locations.

3. The ANOVA tests are used any time we need to compare more than two categories, for example, if we need to compare three sales locations. One thing to remember is that in an ANOVA, if the null hypothesis is rejected, it means that at least one of the means are different. It does not, however, tell you which one is different. ANOVA is really just a multi-input *t*-test.

Table 7.3 Continuous data hypothesis test selection table.

Situation	Tool
One sample versus historic average	One-sample *t*-test
Sample from each of two processes	Two-sample *t*-test
Samples from three or more processes	ANOVA

The upcoming examples of these three common hypothesis tests are meant as refresher examples and are not intended to completely teach the proper use of the tool. There are many sources for performing the actual calculation including textbooks and software such as MINITAB. The purpose of this text is to supplement the reader's learning by providing examples of the application of Six Sigma tools at the proper point in the progression of the project. While it is important to understand the statistical calculations to some degree, the Green Belt does not need to be overly concerned with why a tool works. After all, you do not need to be a mechanical engineer to drive a car.

One-Sample *t*-Test

The one-sample *t*-test is used when we want to compare a sample from a new or different process to a historical mean or known value. In our drive to work example, we know that the average drive to work time is 20 minutes from data collected over the last year. We have since discovered that there is a new route, and we would like to determine if the alternate route is any different than our current route. To answer this question, we use the alternate route for the next five days, record the drive time, and compare those samples to our historic mean using the one-sample *t*-test. The drive times are recorded as 17, 23, 18, 20, and 19 minutes.

The null hypothesis is that the drive time on the original route is equal to the drive time on the alternate route, written as:

H_0: original route = new route

This leaves the alternate hypothesis as the drive time on the original route is not equal to the drive time on the alternate route. Written as:

H_a: original route ≠ new route

While not completely statistically correct, in Six Sigma we say that either one or the other is true. So either the drive time on the original route is equal to the drive time on the new route or the drive time on the original route is not equal to the drive time on the alternate route. If the drive times on the two routes are not equal, this means that one is shorter than the other, which in this case would be desirable.

Table 7.4 Sample data used in *t*-test.

Individual	Average	Ind. – Avg.	(Ind. – Avg.)²
17	19.4	–2.4	5.76
23	19.4	3.6	12.96
18	19.4	–1.4	1.96
20	19.4	0.6	0.36
19	19.4	–0.4	0.16
		Sum	21.2

To perform the one-sample *t*-test, we need to calculate a *t*-value for our sample and compare that *t*-value to a tabulated *t*-value called the *critical t*. The critical *t* is based on the degrees of freedom, which is $n - 1$ (the number of samples –1). If the calculated *t*-value is less than the tabulated *t*-value, we accept the null hypothesis and say the old route and new route are equal. If the calculated *t*-value is greater than the tabulated *t*-value, we reject the null hypothesis and say the alternate is true and the routes are not equal. Table 7.4 organizes our data.

The *t*-value is calculated using the following:

$$t = \frac{sample\,average - historic\,mean}{\left(\dfrac{\sigma}{\sqrt{sample\,size}}\right)}$$

The sample average is $\dfrac{17 + 23 + 18 + 20 + 19}{5} = 19.4$

The historic mean is 20, from the example.

The sample standard deviation is $\sqrt{\dfrac{\sum\left(individual - average\right)^2}{n - 1}}$

Standard deviation $= \sqrt{\dfrac{21.2}{5 - 1}} = 2.30$

Calculated $t = \dfrac{19.4 - 20}{\dfrac{2.3}{\sqrt{5}}} = -0.58$

To determine critical t, look value up in table for four degrees of freedom, two-tailed test 95% confidence in a standard t-distribution table.

Critical $t = 3.495$

Since –0.58 is less than 3.495, we do not have enough evidence to reject the null hypothesis. We conclude that the new route is no different from the original route. If the calculated t-value were larger than the critical, we would have rejected the null hypothesis and said that the alternate route was different from the original route and concluded that one is actually shorter than the other.

Software packages will return a p-value. If the p-value is less than 0.05, the null hypothesis is rejected and you say there is a difference; if the p-value is greater than 0.05, the null is not rejected and you say there is no difference. This is true for all of the hypothesis tests discussed.

Two-Sample *t*-Test

In the preceding case, if we wished to compare two alternate routes and we collect a sample of drive times from each, the t-test changes slightly and we would use a two-sample t-test. This test works the same as the one-sample t-test, but instead of comparing one sample to a historic mean we compare two samples. For example, we have alternate route A with drive times of 17, 23, 18, 20, and 19 minutes and alternate route B with drive times of 26, 24, 23, 26, and 28. The question we ask is, are the routes the same?

The null hypothesis is:

H_0: Route A = Route B

The alternate hypothesis is:

H_a: Route A ≠ Route B

The calculated *t*-value is given by:

$$t = \frac{Average_{RouteA} - Average_{RouteB}}{\sqrt{\dfrac{s_{1^2}^2}{n_1} + \dfrac{s_2^2}{n_2}}}$$

$$t = \frac{19.4 - 25.4}{\sqrt{\dfrac{2.3^2}{5} + \dfrac{1.95^2}{5}}} = -4.45$$

This value must be compared to the critical *t* values from the *t*-table. To get this we need to calculate the degrees of freedom. In a two-sample *t*-test, degrees of freedom are given by $df = n_1 + n_2 - 2$, which is $5 + 5 - 2 = 8$. From the table for a two-tailed test at 95% confidence and eight degrees of freedom, the critical *t*-value is 2.306, Since the absolute value of the calculated *t* is greater than the value of the tabulated *t*, we reject the null hypothesis and conclude that there is a difference in the average drive times between route A and route B.

Note that this example assumes equal variances. Figure 7.3 shows a MINITAB analysis of route A and route B. Since the *p* value is less than 0.005, we also conclude that there is a difference between route A and route B.

```
Two-Sample T-Test and CI: RouteA, RouteB

Two-sample T for RouteA vs RouteB

          N    Mean   StDev   SE Mean
RouteA    5   19.40    2.30      1.0
RouteB    5   25.40    1.95      0.87


Difference = mu (RouteA) - mu (RouteB)
Estimate for difference:   -6.00000
95% CI for difference:  (-9.11097, -2.88903)
T-Test of difference = 0 (vs not =): T-Value = -4.45
                                     P-Value = 0.002   DF = 8
Both use Pooled StDev = 2.1331
```

Figure 7.3   Two-sample *t*-test and CI: route A, route B.

ANOVA

Analysis of variance (ANOVA) is a special application of the two-sample *t*-test that can be applied to more than two samples. If, for example, in our drive to work problem we wished to compare three or more routes, we would use ANOVA. Given the following data set, we wish to determine if there is a difference in any of the three routes. Our null hypothesis becomes:

H_0: Route A = Route B = Route C

The alternate hypothesis is:

H_a: At least one of the route averages is different

In ANOVA we compare the variance of each treatment average (the overall average) or route, in this case, to the variance of the error term, which is the variance of each observation to the treatment or group average. In general, we say that if the treatment variance is large relative to the error variance, at least one of the treatments is different. This comparison is made by comparing a calculated *F* value and a tabulated *F* value, much like the *t*-test compares *t*-values. The variance is also equal to the sum of squares (*SS*) divided by the degrees of freedom (*df*), also called the mean square (*MS*).

To make this comparison we need to determine five items:

1. Sum of squares (*SS*): group, error, and total

2. Degrees of freedom (*df*)

3. Mean square (*MS*)

4. *F* calculated

5. *F* tabulated

We first start by calculating the average of each group and the average of the samples. See Table 7.5.

The group *SS* is calculated by subtracting the average of each group from the overall average, squaring the result, and adding them up and multiplying by the number of samples per group. See Table 7.6. This is written as

$$SS_{Group} = n \times \sum \left(GroupAverage - OverallAverage \right)^2$$

Table 7.5 ANOVA sample data.

	Route A	Route B	Route C
Time 1	17	28	16
Time 2	23	26	15
Time 3	18	24	17
Time 4	20	23	18
Time 5	19	26	21
Average	19.4	25.4	17.4
Overall average	20.73		

Table 7.6 Group sum of squares calculation table.

Group	Group Average	Overall Average	Difference	Difference^2
Route A	19.4	20.73	−1.33	1.778
Route B	25.4	20.73	4.67	21.778
Route C	17.4	20.73	−3.33	11.111
			Sum of diff. squared	34.67
			Samples per group	5
			SS group	34.67 × 5 = 173.4

The error sum of squares is calculated by summing the squared differences between each individual and its group mean and then adding the totals to get the sum of squares for the error term. See Table 7.7. This is written as:

$$\sum^{Groups} \sum^{Individuals} \left(Individuals - GroupAverage\right)^2$$

The total sum of squares is calculated by summing the squared differences of each individual value as compared to the overall average of the data. See Table 7.8. This is written as:

$$\sum \left(Individuals - OverallAverage\right)^2$$

Table 7.7   Sums of squares calculation table.

Route A	Group Avg.	Difference	Difference²	SS
17	19.4	−2.4	5.76	
23	19.4	3.6	12.96	
18	19.4	−1.4	1.96	
20	19.4	0.6	0.36	
19	19.4	−0.4	0.16	
		Total Route A		21.2
Route B				
28	25.4	2.6	6.76	
26	25.4	0.6	0.36	
24	25.4	−1.4	1.96	
23	25.4	−2.4	5.76	
26	25.4	0.6	0.36	
		Total Route B		15.2
Route C				
16	17.4	−1.4	196	
15	17.4	−2.4	5.76	
17	17.4	−0.4	0.16	
18	17.4	0.6	0.36	
21	17.4	3.6	12.96	
		Total Route C		21.2
		Error sum of squares		57.6

Degrees of freedom (df) need to be calculated for the group, error, and total sum of squares as follows:

df group = Number of groups − 1 = 3 − 1 = 2

df error = (Number of data points − 1) − (Number of groups − 1) = (15 − 1) − (3 − 1) = 12

df total SS = Number of data points − 1 = 15 − 1 = 14

At this point the ANOVA table can be completed to determine the F value, which will allow us to either accept or reject the null

Table 7.8 Total sum of squares calculation table.

Route A	Overall Average	Difference	Difference²	SS
17	20.73	−3.73	13.91	
23	20.73	2.27	5.15	
18	20.73	−2.73	7.45	
20	20.73	−0.73	.53	
19	20.73	−1.73	2.99	
			Total Route A	30.03
Route B				
28	20.73	7.27	52.85	
26	20.73	5.27	27.77	
24	20.73	3.27	10.69	
23	20.73	2.27	5.15	
26	20.73	5.27	27.77	
			Total Route B	124.23
Route C				
16	20.73	−4.73	22.37	
15	20.73	−5.73	32.83	
17	20.73	−3.73	13.91	
18	20.73	−2.73	7.45	
21	20.73	0.27	0.07	
			Total Route C	76.63
			Total sum of squares	231

hypothesis. The *SS* and *df* values are transferred from the previous calculations. The mean square is calculated by dividing the *SS* by *df*. *F* (calc) is determined by dividing the group mean square by the error mean square. *F* (tabulated) is taken from an *F* distribution table. In this case, $\alpha = 0.05$ with two *df* in the numerator and 12 *df* in the denominator, which is 3.89. Since the *F* calculated is greater than *F* tabulated, we reject the null hypothesis. This indicates that at least one of the route average drive times is different. In practical terms, this means that at least one route takes less time.

Table 7.9 ANOVA table used to calculate the *F* value.

Source	SS	df	Mean Square	F (calc)	F (tabulated)
Group	173.4	2	173.4 / 2 = 86.7	86.7 / 4.8 = 18.06	3.89
Error	57.6	12	57.6 / 12 = 4.8		
Total	231	14			

Table 7.10 Excel ANOVA ouput.

ANOVA: Single Factor

SUMMARY

Groups	Count	Sum	Average	Variance
Route A	5	97	19.4	5.3
Route B	5	127	25.4	3.8
Route C	5	87	17.4	5.3

ANOVA

Source of Variation	SS	df	MS	F	P-value	F crit
Between Groups	173.3333	2	86.66667	18.05556	0.000241	3.885294
Within Groups	57.6	12	4.8			
Total	230.9333	14				

To get the *F* calculated value, an ANOVA table must be constructed. See Table 7.9.

The same analysis could be performed in MINITAB using the one-way ANOVA function or in Excel using one-factor ANOVA in the data analysis tool pack. See Table 7.10. Figure 7.4 gives the MINITAB analysis of the previous example.

There are several specialized types of ANOVA hypothesis tests available. The selection of the proper test is determined by the situation and the question the Green Belt is attempting to answer. Table 7.11, ANOVA selection table, lists typical ANOVA situations and the proper ANOVA tool to use. If you were going to compare processing cost of three claim centers, this would be one treatment (claim center) at three levels and according to the table, the one-way ANOVA is the proper type of ANOVA to use.

```
One-way ANOVA: Stacked versus subs

Source    DF      SS      MS      F      P
subs       2  173.33   86.67  18.06  0.000
Error     12   57.60    4.80
Total     14  230.93

S = 2.191   R-Sq = 75.06%   R-Sq(adj) = 70.90%


                              Individual 95% CIs For Mean Based on
                              Pooled StDev
Level      N    Mean   StDev ------+---------+---------+---------+---
Route A    5  19.400   2.302      (-----*------)
Route B    5  25.400   1.949                     (------*-----)
Route C    5  17.400   2.302 (-----*-----)
                              ------+---------+---------+---------+---
                              17.5      21.0      24.5      28.0
```

Figure 7.4 One-way ANOVA: stacked versus subs.

Table 7.11 ANOVA selection table.

Situation	ANOVA to Use
One treatment at multiple levels of response	One-way ANOVA
Two treatments at multiple levels of response	Two-way ANOVA
Multiple treatments at multiple responses where all treatment combinations have the same number of observations (Balanced)	Balanced ANOVA
Multiple treatments at multiple responses, not required to be balanced	General linear model

In both the MINITAB and Excel examples, the p-value is less than 0.05 and the null hypothesis is rejected. This indicates that at least one of the means is different, which is the same result as from the manual calculation. See Table 7.11.

CONTINUOUS INPUT AND CONTINUOUS OUTPUT

In cases where we have both a continuous input variable and continuous output variable and we need to verify that there is or is not a relationship between the two, correlation and regression tools are required. *Correlation* is the degree of linear association between two variables and ranges from −1 to +1, and is denoted by r. What this means is that if we have $r = +1$ we have perfect positive correlation. If $r = -1$, there is perfect negative correlation, and if r is zero, there is no correlation. The r value can be anywhere from −1 to +1, so you could also have an r of, say, 0.7. See Figure 7.5. A positive correlation means that the input variable (predictor) increases in value as the output variable (response) also increases in value. A negative correlation is the opposite case, where as the input variable increases the output variable decreases. No correlation is the case where the input variable can not be used to predict the output.

Correlation tells us if the relationship exists. This is important in a Six Sigma project because, as we sort through the various process inputs and outputs, we need to determine which of the inputs have a significant impact on the output. We need to know this relationship so that the significant inputs can be controlled and the process output can be predicted.

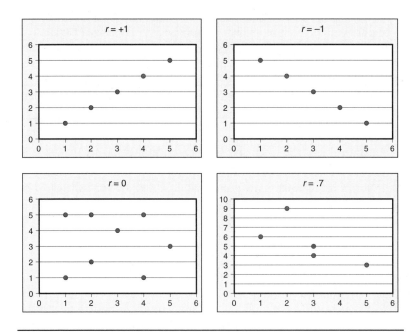

Figure 7.5 Graphs indicating various r values.

Table 7.12   Data table for calls in queue versus wait time.

Calls in Queue	Wait Time (Secs)
2	60
4	80
6	100
8	120

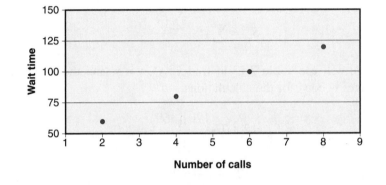

Figure 7.6   Graph of calls versus wait time.

Just imagine drawing a straight line that best fits the points on the graph and *r* is the degree to which those points are linearly related. If the line slopes up and to the right and all points fall on the line, *r* = 1, which is shown in the upper left corner of Figure 7.5.

As an example, let's assume a situation where call waiting time increases as the number of calls in the queue increases. Table 7.12 organizes the data. Figure 7.6 demonstrates the *r* value.

From the table and chart we see that for every two additional calls in the queue, the wait time increases by 20 seconds. So, in our example, the wait time is associated or correlated with the number of calls in the queue. This is fine, but we need a measure of this correlation, so we use something called the Pearson's correlation coefficient, denoted by *r* and named after the person who came up with it. This can be calculated as follows:

$$r = \sum (x - \bar{x})(y - \bar{y}) / \sqrt{\sum (x - \bar{x})^2 (y - \bar{y})^2}$$

This is actually equal to $\dfrac{S_{xy}}{\sqrt{S_{x^2}S_{y^2}}}$

Where:

$$S_{xy} = \sum xy - \frac{\sum x \sum y}{n}$$

$$S_{x^2} = \sum x^2 - \frac{\sum(x^2)}{n}$$

$$S_{y^2} = \sum y^2 - \frac{\sum(y^2)}{n}$$

We will use Table 7.13 to find x^2, y^2, $x \times y$, and the sums and averages needed for the calculations.

$$S_{xy} = 2000 - \frac{(20)(360)}{4} = 200$$

$$S_{x^2} = 120 - \frac{20^2}{4} = 20$$

$$S_{y^2} = 3440 - \frac{360^2}{4} = 2000$$

We are almost there. Just plug the values into the original equation,

$$r = \frac{S_{xy}}{\sqrt{S_{x^2}S_{y^2}}} = \frac{20}{\sqrt{(20)(2000)}} = 1$$

Table 7.13 Regression calculation table.

	Calls (x)	Time (y)	x^2	y^2	$x \times y$
	2	60	4	3600	120
	4	80	16	6400	320
	6	100	36	10000	600
	8	120	64	14400	960
Sum (Σ)	20	360	120	34400	2000
Avg ($\bar{x}$)	5	90			

So in this case, we say we have a perfect positive correlation or an $r = 1$.

Regression is very similar to correlation, but provides much more information. In regression, we attempt to fit a line to the data and develop an equation for that line. This allows us to predict the y value if we know the x value, so if we knew the number of calls in the queue we could predict wait time.

If you remember from high school algebra that an equation for a line is $y = mx + b$, we can use what we have already done to find our regression line. The line is fitted by a method known as *least squares*.

In our case, we want to predict y, so we will need to calculate m and b and then plug in our x value. We find m and b as follows:

$$m = \frac{S_{xy}}{S_{x^2}}$$

$$b = \bar{y} - \left(\frac{S_{xy}}{S_{x^2}}\right)\bar{x}$$

So we have:

$$m = \frac{200}{20} = 10$$

$$b = 90 - \left(\frac{200}{20}\right)5 = 40$$

Now plug and chug:

$$y = mx + b, \text{ so}$$

$$y = 10(x) + 40$$

With this we can predict the wait based on the calls in the queue. So if there are three calls in the queue, the wait time will be $y = mx + b$ or wait time $= 10 \times 3 + 40$, which equals 70. So with three calls in the queue we will expect to wait 70 seconds.

All models will not be perfect fits like our example (all points in a straight line). To address this we use something called the *coefficient of determination,* or r^2. This value describes the amount of the y variable that can be explained by changes in the x variable. To find this, we square the correlation coefficient, in our example, $1^2 = 1$ or 100% of the y is explained by the x variable. If the correlation coefficient was 0.8, then $0.8^2 = 0.64$ or 64% would be explained. The higher the number the better the equation models the data.

In most cases, software will be used to calculate correlation coefficients and regression equations. The example was given here to provide an understanding of how the calculation works.

A word of caution on using regression: You must be very careful when predicting values outside of your data range. For example, think about the relationship of a person's height to age. In the early years, it would seem that as age increases so does height; however, using that data to predict height past the age of 16 or 18 would indicate that you would be 10 feet tall at some point! Regression is a very powerful tool and can be used to define many relationships that will assist in solving quality problems and improving processes; just understand what you are trying to predict and always do a sanity check on your results.

Figure 7.7 shows MINITAB analysis using fitted line plot. Excel output for the same data is shown in Table 7.14.

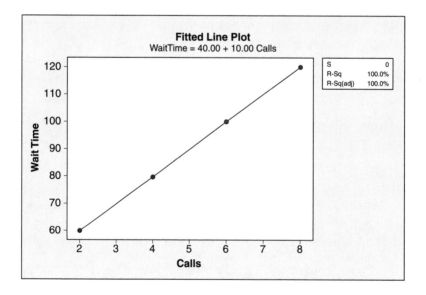

Figure 7.7 MINITAB fitted line plot output for wait time versus call data.

Table 7.14 Excel output for wait time versus call data.

SUMMARY OUTPUT

Regression Statistics

Multiple R	1
R Square	1
Adjusted R Square	1
Standard Error	0
Observations	4

ANOVA

	df	SS	MS	F	Significance F
Regression	1	2000	2000	0	
Residual	2	0	0		
Total	3	2000			

	Coefficients	Standard Error	t Stat	P-value	Lower 95%	Upper 95%	Lower 95.0%	Upper 95.0%
Intercept	40	0	65535		40	40	40	40
X Variable 1	10	0	65535		10	10	10	10

CATEGORICAL INPUT VERSUS ATTRIBUTE OUTPUT

In the case of categorical inputs and attribute outputs, let's say, for example, that you wanted to compare the percentage of dissatisfied customers by category. There are two tests available, and like *t*-tests and ANOVA, the choice is dependent on what you are comparing.

If you are comparing a historic percentage of dissatisfied customers to the percent of dissatisfied customers after a change or process improvement, you would use the one-proportion test. If you are comparing summarized data (number of customers versus number dissatisfied) from more than two locations, the cross-tabulation table of a chi-squared table would be used. See Table 7.15.

One-Proportion Test

Let's say, for example, you wanted to compare the credit denial rates (measured in proportions) between a single location and a known historic proportion. The one-proportion test could be used. When the conditions are met that the sample size is greater than 30 and $n(1 - p) > 5$, the binominal approximation to the normal distribution can be used. In other cases, the Green Belt should use software or consult a statistical text on the subject. In our example we have:

Historic proportion $(P) = 0.1$

A sample (n) of 100 is taken and seven applications are denied.

H_0: Historic proportion = Sample proportion

H_a: Historic proportion $\neq$ Sample proportion

Table 7.15   Categorical input versus attribute output.

Situation	Tool
Sample proportion versus historic proportion	One-proportion test
Summarized data from two or more populations or samples	Cross-tabulation table (chi-squared table)

```
Test and CI for One Proportion

Test of p = 0.1 vs p not = 0.1


Sample  X    N   Sample p         95% CI          Z-Value  P-Value
1       7   100  0.070000  (0.019992, 0.120008)   -1.00    0.317
```

Figure 7.8 Test and CI for one proportion.

Our test Z value is ± 1.96 (alpha 0.05) from the Z table. The test requires that we determine a calculated Z value and compare it to the tabulated Z values for the required alpha risk.

$$\text{Calculates } Z = Z = \frac{p - P}{\sqrt{\dfrac{P(1-P)}{n}}} = \frac{0.07 - 0.1}{\sqrt{\dfrac{0.1(1-0.1)}{100}}} = \frac{-0.03}{\sqrt{\dfrac{0.09}{100}}} = -1$$

Comparing -1 to the test Z of ± 1.96, the calculated Z is less than the tabulated Z, so the null hypothesis is not rejected and we conclude there is a not a difference between the sample and the historic proportion.

The test can be performed in MINITAB with the results shown in Figure 7.8. Since the *p*-value is greater than 0.05, the null is not rejected, as in the manual example.

Chi-Squared Table

When comparing proportions from two or more samples, the chi-square statistic is used. This involves comparing the observed proportions to the proportion expected if there were no differences between the samples. If the observed result is greater than the expected result, we reject the null hypothesis and say there is a significant difference in the sample proportions. This test can be thought of as the binominal version of the ANOVA test discussed earlier.

Say, for example, we have three call centers and wish to determine if the customer complaint level is different at any of the three locations. The data collected are in the form of numbers of calls handled

Table 7.16 Complaints versus call raw data.

Call Center	Total Calls	Total Calls without Complaints	Total Complaints
A	230	215	15
B	125	116	9
C	418	401	17

versus the number of customer complaints for a given period of time. Table 7.16 organizes the data.

The null hypothesis for this test is that there is no difference and the alternate is that there is a difference in at least one of the call centers.

H_0: Call center A = call center B = call center C

H_a: At least one call center is different

Convert the data into a summarized table for calculation. Table 7.17 is an example.

Determine expected values for each column and row combination. Expected values (call center A without complaints) =

$$\frac{RawTotal \times ColumnTotal}{GrandTotal} = \frac{732 \times 230}{773} = 217.8$$

Expected values (call center B without complaints) =

$$\frac{RawTotal \times ColumnTotal}{GrandTotal} = \frac{732 \times 125}{773} = 118.37$$

Expected values (call center C without complaints) =

$$\frac{RowTotal \times ColumnTotal}{GrandTotal} = \frac{732 \times 418}{773} = 395.83$$

Expected values (call center A with complaints) =

$$\frac{RowTotal \times ColumnTotal}{GrandTotal} = \frac{41 \times 230}{773} = 12.20$$

Table 7.17 Summarized data table.

	A	**B**	**C**	**Total**
Calls without complaints	215	116	401	732
Complaints	15	9	17	41
Total	230	125	418	773

Expected values (call center B with complaints) =

$$\frac{Row Total \times Column Total}{Grand Total} = \frac{41 \times 125}{773} = 6.63$$

Expected values (call center C with complaints) =

$$\frac{Row Total \times Column Total}{Grand Total} = \frac{41 \times 418}{773} = 22.17$$

Calculate the total chi-square value by summing individual chi-square values from each column/row combination:

$$x^2 = \sum \frac{(O-E)^2}{E}$$

$$x^2 = \frac{(215 - 217.8)^2}{217.8} + \frac{(116 - 118.37)^2}{118.37} + \frac{(401 - 395.83)^2}{395.83}$$

$$+ \frac{(15 - 12.20)^2}{12.20} + \frac{(9 - 6.63)^2}{6.63} + \frac{(17 - 22.17)^2}{22.17}$$

$$= 0.036 + 0.047 + 0.068 + 0.643 + 0.847 + 1.206 = 2.847$$

Calculate the degrees of freedom in order to determine the critical chi-square value:

$$\text{Degrees of freedom} = (\text{rows} - 1)(\text{Columns} - 1)$$
$$= (2 - 1)(3 - 1) = 2$$

From the chi-squared table at two degrees of freedom, alpha = 0.05, the critical value is 5.99. The value can also be obtained using Excel function CHIINV(alpha,dF)

```
Chi-Square Test: A, B, C

Expected counts are printed below observed counts
Chi-Square contributions are printed below expected counts

              A        B        C   Total
    1       215      116      401     732
         217.80   118.37   395.83
          0.036    0.047    0.068

    2        15        9       17      41
          12.20     6.63    22.17
          0.643    0.847    1.206

Total      230      125      418     773

Chi-Sq = 2.847, DF = 2, P-Value = 0.241
```

Figure 7.9 Chi-square test: A, B, C.

Since the calculated chi-square is less than the critical chi-square, we can not reject the null hypothesis, so we conclude there is not a significant difference in customer complaints between the call centers. Figure 7.9 shows the MINITAB analysis.

Since the *p*-value is greater than 0.05, we can not reject the null hypothesis, so we say that there is no difference in the number of complaints between the call centers. This is the same result as before.

SAMPLE SIZES

A very common question when using sample data to make a decision concerning a process is, how many samples should I take? The real answer to this question is that it depends. It depends on the amount of variation in the population, what the meaningful difference is, how much risk we are willing to take in our decision. If you recall our discussion on hypothesis testing, there is an alpha and beta risk associated with each statistical decision. Typically the alpha is set to 0.05 and the beta set at 0.10. The variation is determined by the process, which we may or may not know. The meaningful difference could be considered the minimum amount of change needed before we would make a decision. To put it another way, if you had to choose between claims software A, which is already installed and in use, and claims software B, which is the new and improved version, how much better does software B need to be before you will upgrade? Does it have to be 10% faster or 100% faster? There again it depends on the process.

One problem with sample size selection is that you need to know the variation in the process and many times you do not. Variation is important because as the variation increases, given all other factors are constant, the sample size must increase to detect a given meaningful difference. If you think about comparing populations and each had zero variation, you could do this with one sample from each group, as the sample would perfectly represent the average of the population. This, of course, is never actually the case. Software packages such as MINITAB will calculate sample sizes given the variation in terms of standard deviation, meaningful difference, and alpha and beta risks. (Beta is also referred to as 1–power.) Figure 7.10 shows a sample-size calculation screen from MINITAB for a two-sample *t*-test.

Sample-size selection also depends on the test you are using and the type of data you are using to make the decision. In many cases

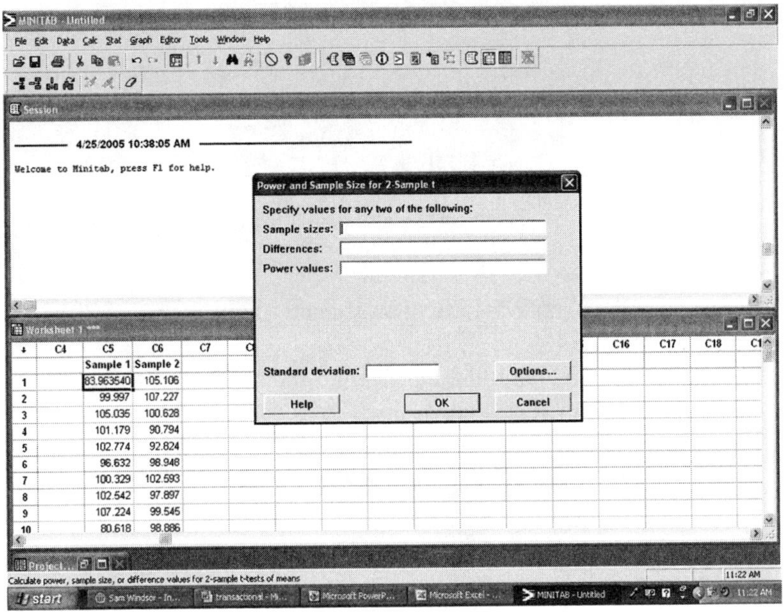

Figure 7.10   Sample-size calculation screen.

manual calculation of sample size is beyond the scope of this text; however, a simple example is useful in helping the student understand the concept. In a continuous data example, we wish to determine the sample size required to detect a difference of one unit when the standard deviation of the process is two units with a confidence of 95%. (Note: This example only considers the alpha risk.)

From the Z table, 95% equates to a Z of 1.96. We are given a difference (δ) and a standard deviation (σ) of one. The sample size becomes:

$$N = (Z^2 \times \sigma^2) / \delta^2 = (1.96^2 \times 2^2) / 1^2 = 15.36$$

Since the sample needs to be whole numbers, round up to 16.

Now, consider an example sample size for a two-sample *t*-test when both alpha and beta risk are considered. Given an alpha (α) of 0.05 and a beta (β) of 0.10 (power = 0.90), the standard deviation (σ) of two and difference (δ) of two, the sample size is given by

$$n = 2\left[\left(Z_{\frac{\alpha}{2}} + Z_\beta\right)^2\right]\frac{\sigma^2}{\delta^2}$$

$$n = 2\left[\left(1.96 + 1.28\right)^2\right]\frac{2^2}{2^2}$$

$$n = 20.995$$

$Z_{\frac{\alpha}{2}} = 1.96$, from Z tale 0.025 (inverse cumulative probability)

$Z_\beta = 1.28$, from Z tale 0.9 (inverse cumulative probability)

A statistics text should be consulted for further information.

RESIDUAL ANALYSIS

In cases where a model is used to describe a data set, there will be a difference between the predicted value of the model and the actual data. This difference is called the *residual*. Residual analysis is a useful tool in determining the usefulness of the model. Residual analysis helps to determine if the model is adequate to define the relationship between an independent and dependent variable.

For example, let's take the following data set and perform a regression analysis in MINITAB, as Figure 7.11 shows.

Raw Data	
X	**Y**
20	0.2021
25	0.5654
30	1.8469
35	1.9149
40	2.4617
45	7.1984
50	9.4572
55	15.7317
60	20.7835

From the plot in Figure 7.11 you can see that the data deviate from the fitted line. Using the residual analysis graphs generated in MINITAB, see Figure 7.12, you can see from the histogram that the residuals are not normally distributed. Also by looking at the graph in the upper right hand corner you see that from –5 through zero the residuals are positive; from zero to 12 the residuals are negative; and

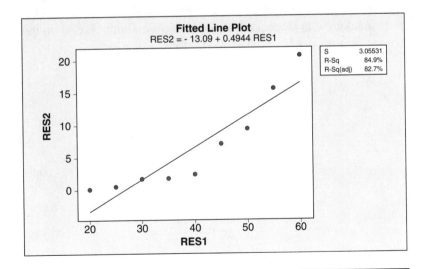

Figure 7.11 Fitted line plot from MINITAB.

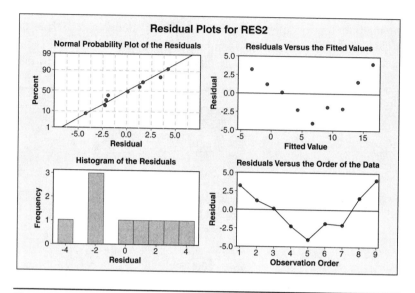

Figure 7.12   Residual analysis from MINITAB.

above 15 the residuals are positive again. If the model was a good model of the relationship between X and Y, we would expect the residuals to be normally distributed and random when plotted against the fitted value. The chart Residual versus Observation Order also indicates a problem with the data as you would expect the residuals to be random with respect to the order of observation. Based on this, the model may not be the best model for the data set:

X	Y
20	100.761
25	100.910
30	101.090
35	101.483
40	102.198
45	102.209
50	102.581
55	102.908
60	103.127
65	103.410

In this case, the residuals are normally distributed and appear to be in random order about the fitted line. Figure 7.13 shows this. In residual analysis, you are looking for extreme patterns; minor deviations from what you expect are not uncommon given small data sets. Figure 7.14 shows this.

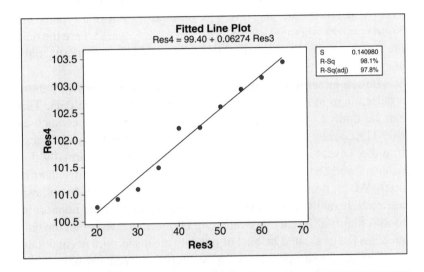

Figure 7.13   Fitted line plot from MINITAB.

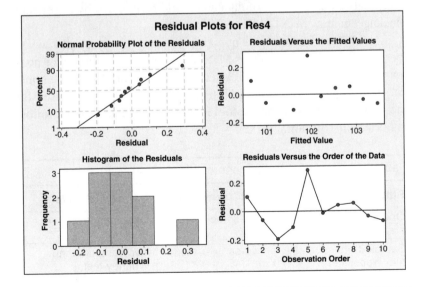

Figure 7.14   Regression analysis from MINITAB.

NONNORMAL DATA

The tools discussed to this point nearly all require data to be normally distributed or to have come from normally distributed population for accurate data analysis. The problem is that in a typical Six Sigma project you may, in fact, encounter many cases where the data are not normally distributed. The tools required to properly make statistical decisions will be discussed in this section.

Before either normal or nonnormal data analysis tools are used, a determination must be made as to the normality of the data. This can be done using a normality test in software packages such as MINITAB or by applying a normal distribution goodness-of-fit test. In either case, the null hypothesis is that the data are normally distributed, and the alternate is that the data are not normally distributed. When nonnormal data are encountered during hypothesis testing, it is really a matter of substituting the appropriate nonnormal tool. A major difference in evaluating nonnormal data is that the data medians are evaluated instead of the data means as with normal data.

The details of nonnormal data analysis are typically beyond the scope of most Green Belt courses. Should nonnormal data be encountered, the local Black Belt or Master Black Belt should be consulted. The analysis of this type of data can easily be handled by a software package such as MINITAB.

Normal and nonnormal hypothesis tests are very similar when performed in software such as MINITAB. Proper nonnormal, or nonparametric as it is called, tool selection is based on the situation just as with normal data. Table 7.18 lists the situation, the tool used for normal data analysis, and the tool to be used if the data do not follow a normal distrition.

Table 7.18 Normal versus nonnormal hypothesis test tools.

Situation	Tool Normal Data	Nonnormal Data
One sample versus historic average	One-sample *t*-test	One-sample sign test
Sample from each of two processes	Two-sample *t*-test	Two-sample Mann Whitney test
Samples from three or more processes	ANOVA	Kruskal-Wallis

Key Points

1. Hypothesis testing is used to determine if there is a difference between inputs.

2. The null hypothesis is stated as, "No difference," and the alternate is stated as "There is a difference."

3. In manual tests, a calculated value is compared to a tabulated value. If the calculated value is greater than the tabulated value, the null is rejected.

4. Using software, if the *p*-value is less than 0.05, the null is rejected.

5. Tests can either compare historic data to a sample (one-sample tests) or compare samples to each other (two-sample tests and ANOVA).

6. ANOVA is used when we wish to compare more than two samples and is really an expansion of a *t*-test.

7. To select the appropriate test, the type of data must first be determined.

8. If samples are not drawn from a normally distributed population, non-parametric (nonnormal) tests should be used.

CHAPTER REFERENCES

Gonick, Larry, and Woollcott Smith. *The Cartoon Guide to Statistics.* New York: HarperPerennial, 1993.

Juran, Joseph M., and A. Blanton Godfrey. *Juran's Quality Handbook.* 5th ed. New York: McGraw-Hill, 1999.

Kiemele, Mark J., Stephen R. Schmidt, and Ronald J. Berbine. *Basic Statistics, Tools for Continuous Improvement.* 4th ed. Colorado Springs, CO: Air Academy Press, 2000.

8

Optimizing the Process

FULL-FACTORIAL DESIGN OF EXPERIMENTS (DOE)

A key tool in determining and quantifying the relationship of the input variable(s) to the output variable(s) is design of experiments (DOE). Although there are many types of designed experiments available, most Green Belt training material focuses on the standard full-factorial design. Modern software packages reduce the work of analyzing DOE data from days to seconds. I will give some explanation of the methods used to analyze DOE data, but do not intend to cover the details of manual analysis. Rather, I will discuss interpretation of software analysis, as this will most likely be the method used.

Up until this point in the Six Sigma project, data have been collected and analyzed to determine if a relationship actually exists using tools such as hypothesis testing, ANOVA, and regression. What we haven't done is intentionally change the inputs to determine the effect on the output. This is what DOE is all about. In a DOE we will expand on the relationship of the inputs to the output, $Y = f(x)$ through the use of a series of designed experiments. The key advantage of DOE over traditional, one-factor-at-a-time experimentation, is that DOE allows you to investigate the effect of interactions of the factor levels. Interactions are important when the optimal process output is the result of a combination of factors and may not lie in the extreme factor settings. There are a few key terms that are important to understand.

A *factor* is an input variable that we will control in the experiment. For example, it could be number of processors, types of claims, service location, or types of service.

A *level* is the setting of the factor. If the factor is claim type, we may have two types of claims, say hospital and doctor's office. Factors set at their high level are labeled 1, while factors set at their low level are labeled −1. High and low values may be arbitrarily set in cases where actual values are not involved.

Response is the measurable result yielded from the process when a combination of factors is run at given levels.

Effect is the difference in response averages when the factors are set at their high value verses their low value.

We may have a simple DOE where we wish to investigate the combination of the number of computers (factor 1) and the number of people (factor 2) that are required to process a certain number of claims (response) in a claims process. In order to run a full-factorial DOE, we will need to run each combination of computers and people and then measure the number of claims each combination processed in a given time. The DOE setup would look like Table 8.1.

This is a two-factor, two-level design and consists of four experimental runs. The process would be set up and run the first time with two computers (factor 1 at the low level) and two people (factor 2 at the low level). The experiment would be run for the specified time and the number of claims processed would be recorded. The next run would be with four computers and two people, run for the same time

Table 8.1 DOE factor level.

Run Number	Number of Computers	Number of People
1	2	2
2	4	2
3	2	4
4	4	4

Table 8.2 DOE data collection table.

Run Number	Number of Computers	Number of People	Number of Claims Processed
1	2	2	30
2	4	2	49
3	2	4	31
4	4	4	51
5	2	2	28
6	4	2	47
7	2	4	33
8	4	4	52

with the results recorded. This process would continue until all the runs were completed. In most cases you also want to replicate the design, that is repeat all of the runs at least once for a total of two runs at each factor setting. By doing this, you can begin to look at the effect of variation on process outputs. So in our case we would repeat the first four runs with the same settings; data could then be analyzed in a software package such as MINITAB. Once the data are collected they may look like Table 8.2.

When using a software package such as MINITAB, the design must be created and the data entered in the appropriate columns before the analysis can be performed. Once the design is analyzed the output will be in the format shown in Figure 8.1.

When analyzing data from the MINITAB output window in Figure 8.1, there are a few things to key in on. The first thing you should look for is the p-value. Like hypothesis testing, the p-value tells us if the factor is significant. If the p-value is less than 0.05, the factor is significant. (Many use 0.10 to determine significance in DOE). In our example, we see that both the number of computers and the number of people are significant to the numbers of claims the system is capable of processing. But the real power of DOE lies in the predication equation. The prediction equation defines $Y = f(x)$ and is derived from the coefficients from the output window as shown in Figure 8.2.

Factorial Fit: Claims Processed versus Computers, People

```
Estimated Effects and Coefficients for Claims Processed
(coded units)

Term               Effect     Coef   SE Coef      T      P
Constant                    40.1250   0.4507   89.03  0.000
Computers         19.2500    9.6250   0.4507   21.36  0.000
People             3.2500    1.6250   0.4507    3.61  0.023
Computers*People   0.2500    0.1250   0.4507    0.28  0.795


S = 1.27475   R-Sq = 99.15%   R-Sq(adj) = 98.52%


Analysis of Variance for Claims Processed (coded units)

Source              DF   Seq SS   Adj SS   Adj MS       F      P
Main Effects         2  762.250  762.250  381.125  234.54  0.000
2-Way Interactions   1    0.125    0.125    0.125    0.08  0.795
Residual Error       4    6.500    6.500    1.625
  Pure Error         4    6.500    6.500    1.625
Total                7  768.875


Estimated Coefficients for Claims Processed using data in
uncoded units

Term                   Coef
Constant            7.50000
Computers           9.25000
People              1.25000
Computers*People   0.125000


Alias Structure
I
Computers
People
Computers*People
```

Figure 8.1 Factorial fit: claims processed versus computers, people.

```
Estimated Coefficients for Claims Processed using data in
uncoded units

Term                   Coef
Constant            7.50000
Computers           9.25000
People              1.25000
Computers*People   0.125000
```

Figure 8.2 MINITAB output coefficients for the designed experiment.

In this case, the prediction equation would be:

Let C = number of computers and P = number of people

$$\text{Numbers of claims} = 7.50 + C \times (9.250) + P \times (1.250) + C \times P \times 0.125$$

So if we wanted to determine how many claims we could process with three computers and two people, let $C = 3$ and $P = 2$ and solve the equation.

$$\begin{aligned}\text{Numbers of claims} &= 7.50 + 3 \times (9.250) + 2 \times (1.250) + \\ &\quad 3 \times 2 \times 0.125 = 7.50 + 27.75 + 2.5 + \\ &\quad 0.75 = 38.5\end{aligned}$$

Note: Only uncoded values can be used directly in the prediction equation. Uncoded values are the actual factor setting levels where coded values scale the values to fit the −1 to +1 scale. Coded values can be used, but first must be converted to actual values.

So with three computers and two people, the system will process about 39 claims. From the coefficients it is easy to see that the number of computers has the greatest effect on the number of claims processed (9.250) compared to a coefficient of 1.250 for the number of people.

It is important to realize that the prediction equation is based on sample data and will contain sampling errors. All results from DOE analysis must be validated through confirmation runs of the process at the optimal factor levels before process changes are made.

Another way to see this is to look at the main effects plot, which is a plot of the average number of claims under each condition. See Figure 8.3.

Although in this case the interaction is not significant, it is useful to look at the interaction plot. See Figure 8.4. Parallel lines indicate that no interaction is present. In the event where the lines are not parallel, an interaction is present. An interaction means that a factor or combination of factors has different effects on the response at different levels. For example, if in Figure 8.5 the response with two people and four computers was lower than the response with four people and two computers, we would say there is an interaction. This is due to the fact that the factor computer has a different effect on the number of claims processed due to the number of people involved in processing those claims.

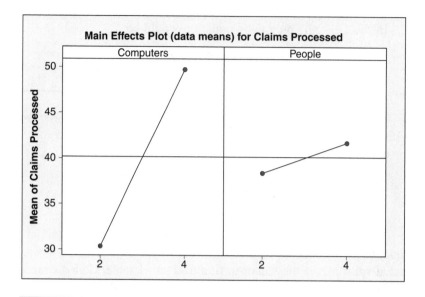

Figure 8.3 MINITAB main effects plots comparing computers and people to number of claims processed.

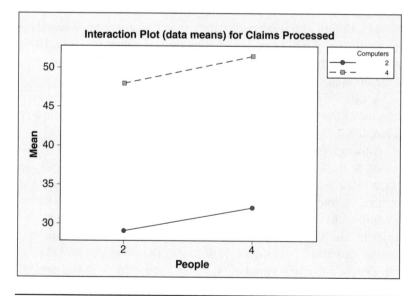

Figure 8.4 MINITAB interaction plot.

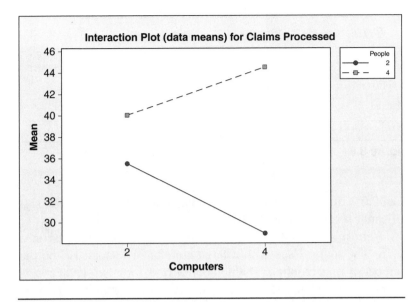

Figure 8.5   Plot showing interactions.

R-SQUARED ADJUSTED

The *R*-squared adjusted value shows the amount of variation explained by this model:

$$S = 1.27475 \quad R\text{-Sq} = 99.15\% \quad R\text{-Sq(adj)} = 98.52\%$$

In this case, the model explains 98.52% of the variation in the experiment, indicating that the model is a good predictor for the process. In general, you will want this value to be 90% or more. Lower values can be used, but the model will describe less of the variation, therefore the model will not be as good of a predictor of the process.

ANOVA TABLE

The *p*-values in the AVOVA table in Figure 8.6 tell us that at least one main effect (people and/or computers) is significant (*p* is less

```
Analysis of Variance for Claims Processed (coded units)

Source                DF    Seq SS    Adj SS    Adj MS       F       P
Main Effects           2   762.250   762.250   381.125   234.54   0.000
2-Way Interactions     1     0.125     0.125     0.125     0.08   0.795
Residual Error         4     6.500     6.500     1.625
  Pure Error           4     6.500     6.500     1.625
Total                  7   768.875
```

Figure 8.6 Analysis of variance for claims processed (coded units).

than 0.05). It also indicates that the interaction of the two is not significant (p is greater than 0.05).

Almost any number of factors and levels could be used in a DOE. The major issue with a large number of factors will be the number of runs required. The number of runs for a two-level experiment can be calculated using L^F, where L is the number of levels and F is the number of factors. With four factors at two levels each, it will require 16 runs (2^4) to complete a full-factorial experiment without replication. The experiment should always be replicated, if possible, which, in this case, will require at least 32 runs.

DOE is a very powerful tool used to determine the optimal factor settings for a process. A DOE should be well thought-out and planned to make the best use of resources, as they are typically expensive to perform. In spite of the expense, an investigation into optimal factor setting can provide huge returns.

Residual analysis is also useful in determining if a model is adequate and is performed in the same manner as when used in regression.

It is beyond the scope of this book to address all the different types and applications of DOE. There are many excellent books that address the topic in great detail. It is important for the Green Belt to understand the basic concepts of DOE in order to understand where a DOE may be applicable.

REGRESSION ANALYSIS

Where both inputs and output are continuous, regression can also be used as an optimization tool. This is done by defining the relationship of inputs to outputs much like the DOE prediction equation. Where multiple inputs are used to predict outputs, multiple regression is performed. Multiple regression data can be analyzed by most any statistical software package.

Key Points

1. DOE is an optimization tool used to develop a prediction equation relating the inputs to the process outputs, $Y = f(x)$.

2. Many types of DOE are available. Selection is based on the available number of runs and levels of interactions to investigate.

3. DOE results must always be confirmed in confirmation runs.

CHAPTER REFERENCES

Douglas, Montgomery. *Design and Analysis of Experiments*. 4th ed. New York: John Wiley and Sons, 1997.

Quality Council of Indiana. *CSSBB Primer*. Terre Haute, IN: Quality Council of Indiana, 2001.

9

Holding the Gains

CONTROL PLANS

Once the process has been fully analyzed, measured, and improved to operate at its optimal point, the biggest mistake we can make is to move on to the next problem before finalizing the one we have been working on. If we leave the project without making some fundamental change in the process, chances are that we will be back in a few months to solve the same problem again. This happens because when process improvements were identified and changes made, there was nothing done to make the changes permanent. If changes are not permanent, the process will slip back to its original state. Control plans are a method to prevent this from happening. The control plan can be developed from the process and the FMEA. Control plan construction steps are as follows:

1. List each step of the process.

2. Identify what is required to perform the process step (resources, computers, data, and so on).

3. Determine the required characteristic(s) of the process step (amount/quality of information, time allotted, and so on).

4. Determine the specification required of the characteristics (minimum/maximum time allotted and minimum/maximum requirements for next process step).

5. Determine frequency and sample size that will be used to verify that the requirement is met (once per day, 100%, and so on).

6. Determine how the data will be monitored (control chart, automated controls, and so on).

7. Determine what will be done if controls are not met (reaction plan).

Let's revisit the first step in our simple process of starting the car. See Figure 9.1. If we think in terms of each of the inputs as a resource and the output as the characteristic and specifications, we can begin to complete the control plan. See Table 9.1.

This example is a very simplified view of the control plan; however, it is useful in illustrating the concept and use of the control plan. Developing the control plan forces you to think through each of the process inputs and determine how the input will be controlled and what will be done if the input exceeds the required specifications. If done correctly, the control plan can even be used to replace the procedure for the process if sufficient information is provided. It is important that the control plan is completed and kept updated in order to ensure that the gains realized during the Six Sigma project are not lost over time.

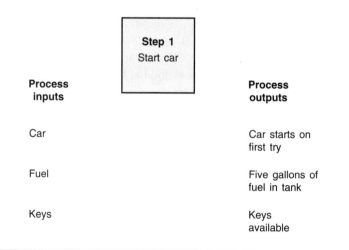

Figure 9.1 One-step process showing inputs and outputs.

Table 9.1 Control for starting the car.

Process Step	Resource	Characteristic	Specification	Sample Size/ Frequency	Control Method	Reaction Plan
Start car	Car	Car must start	Maximum of one attempt	100%	*p*-chart starts on first attempt versus attempts	Send car for tuneup
Start car	Fuel	Quantity of fuel in tank	Minimum five gallons	100%	Fuel gage	Add fuel
Start car	Method to start car	Keys	Keys available 100% of time	100%	*p*-chart for percent of time keys are available	Find keys, determine why keys were not available

CONTROL CHARTS

One method used to control or monitor a process over a period of time is the control chart. The control chart provides a visual indicator of how the current process compares to the process that had been improved during the Six Sigma project. If successful, we brought the average output of the process to a desired target value and implemented methods to control its variation. What we do with a control chart is determine if the current process deviates from the controlled state of the process when the project was completed. This is accomplished by plotting process data on an ongoing basis and comparing the current process to a measure of process centering and process spread from the original process in its controlled state. For example, at the end of a Six Sigma project we have determined that average time to open an account is 20 minutes with a standard deviation of two minutes. If the process is held at this level, the customer will be satisfied. To control this process we have decided to sample five customers per day and record the time required to open their accounts. The *x*-bar and *R* chart in Figure 9.2 was generated.

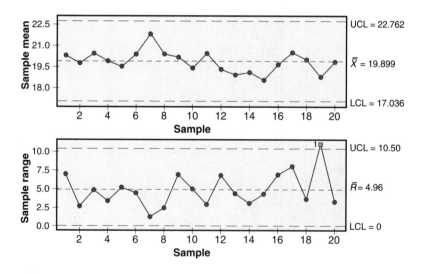

Figure 9.2   *x*-bar and *R* chart plotting time required to open an account.

In this case an *x*-bar and *R* chart was used because we are evaluating subgrouped continuous data. In the first chart, the *x*-bar chart has the average of each subgroup of five plotted. This value is compared to the control limits set at ±3 standard deviations from the averages of the subgroup averages (*x*-double bar). It is important that the mean and control limits are fixed so that new data can be compared to the control limits of the process at the completion of the project. This will allow you to detect any shift in the process average from the established process. There are many rules for monitoring and reacting to control charts. The rules MINITAB uses to indicate that some action is necessary are:

1. One point more than three standard deviations from the centerline

2. Nine points in a row on the same side of the centerline

3. Six points in a row all increasing or decreasing

4. Fourteen points in a row alternating up and down

5. Two of three points greater than two standard deviations from the centerline

6. Four of five points greater than one standard deviation from centerline on same side

7. Fifteen points in a row within one standard deviation from the centerline

8. Eight points in a row greater than one standard deviation from the centerline

The rules vary slightly depending on which text or reference you use, but all are intended to detect a change in the process. Violation of any of the rules is cause for investigation. The theory is that when all points are within the control limits and the rules are not violated, the samples are being drawn from a population that exhibits the parameters of the control chart and nothing in the process has changed from the original state.

There are several other control charts available for use; however the charts shown in Table 9.2 will cover most of the applications a Green Belt will encounter. There are two common charts that are

Table 9.2 Control chart selection.

Data Type	Chart to Use
Subgrouped continuous (measurement)	*X*-bar, *R*, or *X*-bar, sigma
Individual continuous (measurement)	Individual moving range
Binominal	*p*-chart
Discrete (count)	*U* chart

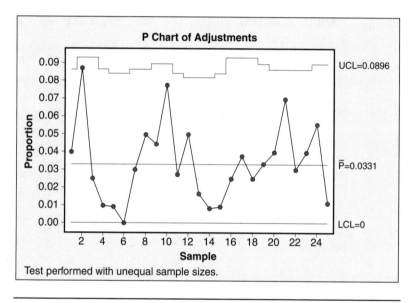

Figure 9.3 Claims requiring adjustment *p*-chart generated in MINITAB.

missing from the preceding data, which are the *np* chart and the *c*-chart. These charts, in my opinion, have been obsoleted by modern software packages. Should software or calculators not be available, and the requirements of constant subgroup sizes be met, the *np* chart could be substituted for the *p*-chart and the *c*-chart could be used in place of the *U* chart.

The *p*-chart shown in Figure 9.3 plots the percentage of claims requiring adjustment in a health claims process. In this particular example, note that the control limits change based on the subgroup sample size.

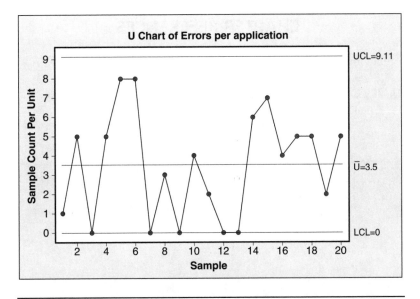

Figure 9.4 *U* chart generated in MINITAB for the number of errors per credit application.

Figure 9.4 shows an example *U* chart tracking errors per application. From the chart you see that the average errors per page is 3.5 with an upper control limit of 9.11 and a lower control limit of zero. This chart is used to monitor the process and as long as the average defects per application is less than 9.11 and no other control rules were violated, nothing has changed in the process. Any data point above 9.11 would indicate that the mean of the process has shifted.

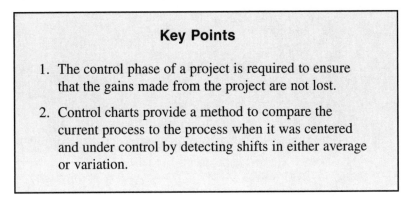

Key Points

1. The control phase of a project is required to ensure that the gains made from the project are not lost.

2. Control charts provide a method to compare the current process to the process when it was centered and under control by detecting shifts in either average or variation.

CHAPTER REFERENCES

Automotive Industry Action Group (AIAG). *Advanced Product Quality Planning and Control Plan* (June 1994).

Quality Council of Indiana. *CSSBB Primer.* Terre Haute, IN: Quality Council of Indiana, 2001.

10

Final Thoughts

It is important to think of Six Sigma as a process for applying statistical tools to analyze data, making decisions about the data, and solving problems. We solve process problems by controlling the centering or target value of the process and reducing process variation to the point where the process output is predictable.

There are no magic bullets in Six Sigma and there is no one tool that solves all problems. Likewise, you will most likely not use all the tools of Six Sigma on any given project. As I said in the very beginning, students need to develop a toolbox and understand how and when to apply each tool at their disposal. The Six Sigma process provides framework and direction to process improvement, but will not in itself make a single process improvement. It is up to the individual to learn the tools and, most importantly, learn how to apply them to solve problems. Often students get so hung up in analyzing data that they forget why they are analyzing data. Remember that data analysis is a means to an end and not the end itself.

In this text I have attempted to cover the questions I hear the most and have attempted to describe the topics that students find the most confusing. The only real way to understand the tools is through hard work and practice. So often students attend a two- or four-week course expecting to come away highly skilled at applying all the tools taught in Six Sigma. This seldom happens. Only through repeated application will you develop the skills and knowledge required. This book is intended to assist the Six Sigma student in developing those skills.

Appendix A is a case study of a Six Sigma project undertaken to reduce employee turnover. Appendix B lists tools commonly used and the associated MINITAB menus and Excel functions to perform those calculations. Appendix C lists common null hypotheses and the corresponding alternate hypotheses.

Appendix A
Case Study

T he following case study represents a portion of a Six Sigma project undertaken to reduce employee turnover. Some sections of the project have been omitted for clarity. The case study is intended to give the reader a real-world example of applying the Six Sigma tools to solve real problems in a nonmanufacturing setting.

A company was faced with an employee turnover rate of 25% per year with about half of the number of employees leaving on their own and the other half being terminated for various reasons. A team was formed consisting of the human resources manager, training manager, two line managers, and a process improvement manager to study and recommend solutions to the turnover issue. The team was charged with reducing the turnover rate to a maximum of 10% by year's end (0.8% per month). The team followed the steps of a Six Sigma process as outlined in Figure 1.1 on page 2.

STEP 1, IDENTIFY OPPORTUNITY
FOR IMPROVEMENT

The cause of pain is defined (25% turnover rate) by management. A cross-functional team is formed to address the issue. The goal for improvement is set by management.

The primary measure of the project was determined to be the turnover rate, so the team was faced with determining the factor that contributed to the current turnover rate of 25%. First the process of recruiting must be understood, so the team developed a process map identifying the inputs and outputs of each process step.

STEP 2, IDENTIFY PROCESS INPUTS AND OUTPUTS USING A PROCESS MAP

The team created a process map, as shown in Figure A.1. Chapter 4 discusses how to create this type of map.

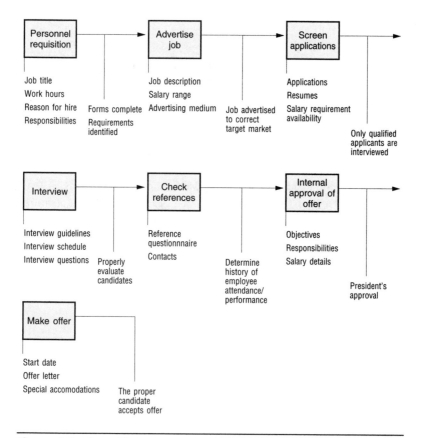

Figure A.1 Recruiting process map.

STEP 3, IDENTIFY PROCESS FAILURE MODES WITH FMEA

Once the process steps are identified, the next step is to determine what can go wrong at each step (that contributes to turnover) using the failure mode and effects analysis tool. The team determined the failure modes from the process map and listed the effects of each failure mode. The failure modes were then rated using severity, occurrence, and detection. See Table A.1. See Chapter 4 for details on how to do this.

The major causes of process failure were that the wrong questions were asked (RPN 720) during the interview process and the objectives and responsibilities were not clearly defined (RPN 420). The cause of asking the wrong questions was believed to be related to variation in questions and variation in the analysis of the interviewee's responses. This led to making offers to candidates who were not qualified or who wouldn't fit the culture of the company. Both conditions will cause increased turnover of employees.

The next highest RPN indicates that the objectives and responsibilities were not completely defined. Not only did this cause a delay in making the offer, it may have caused the employee to be terminated or poorly evaluated if the employee's and manager's expectations were not consistent.

STEP 4, DETERMINE PERFORMANCE MEASURES

The process performance measure was given by management as employee turnover rate. The measure needs to be clearly defined. In this case, it is the total number of employees who left the company either voluntarily or through termination divided by the total number of employees at the end of the evaluation period.

Table A.1 Recruiting process FMEA.

Part/ Process	Failure Mode	Failure Effects	SEV	Causes	OCC	Controls	DET	RPN
Personal requisition	Form incomplete	Req. not approved	8	Manager did not complete form	10	Review by HR	2	160
	Hours not defined	Req. not approved	8	Manager did not complete form	10	Review by HR	2	160
	Reason for opening not stated	Req. not approved	8	Manager did not complete form	10	Review by HR	2	160
	Req. not signed	Req. not approved	8	Manager did not complete form	10	Review by HR	2	160
Advertise	Description incomplete	Wrong person applies	8	No review process	10	Review by manager	1	80
	Job description out of date	Wrong person applies	9	Job not reviewed and updated	8	Periodic review of job descriptions	1	72
	Salary range not given	Incorrect expectations	8	Market value not understood	3	Review by HR	7	168
	Advertise in wrong region	No response	7	No knowledge of area where candidates may be found	5	Review by HR and manager	9	315
	Wrong medium for position	No response	7	Lack of qualified candidates	5	Costs/understanding various mediums	9	315

Continued

Part/Process	Failure Mode	Failure Effects	SEV	Causes	OCC	Controls	DET	RPN
Screening	Required skills not identified	Wrong candidates selected for interview	8	Job requirements not completely defined	10	Reviewed by HR and manager	1	80
	Relevant experience not specified	Wrong candidates selected for interview	8	Related experience not understood	7	Reviewed by HR and manager	1	56
	Education requirements not met	Wrong candidates selected for interview	6	Job requirements not completely defined	2	Reviewed by HR and manager	1	12
	Salary range not determined	Offer not acceptable to candidate	5	Salary range not indicated	5	Reviewed by HR and manager	1	25
	Location specified	Candidate will not relocate	6	Policy not defined	1	Reviewed by HR and manager	1	6
Interview/testing	Candidates not tested or tested correctly for math skills	Basic math skills not present	6	Inadequate assessment criteria	4	Test criteria reviewed by manager	9	216
	Work skills test not properly completed	Candidate unable to perform job	6	Inadequate assessment criteria	4	Test criteria reviewed by manager	9	216
	Candidate's personality not properly evaluated during interview	Candidate may not "fit in"	9	Wrong or inconsistent questions are asked	10	Standard set of questions with standard scoring	8	720

Continued

Continued

Part/ Process	Failure Mode	Failure Effects	SEV	Causes	OCC	Controls	DET	RPN
Interview/ testing	Interviewers not available	Candidate not properly screened	9	Schedule conflicts	5	Better interview scheduling	3	135
Reference check	Limited questions asked or answered	Insufficient info regarding attendance/ job performance	9	References unwilling to disclose certain info	9	Questionnaire	1	81
President's approval	Salary too high	Request refused	8	Salary range not specified on req.	1	Salary to be approved earlier in process	10	80
	Objectives and responsibilities not given	Request refused	7	Info not defined by requesting manager	6	Reviewed by HR before submittal	10	420
Extension of job offer	Salary too low	Below expectations Offer refused	8	Salary range not discussed earlier in process	7	Salary to be approved earlier in process	3	168
	Start date too soon	Start delayed	6	Start date not discussed earlier in process	7	Discuss earlier in process	1	42
	Accommodations not available for candidate	Start delayed	7	Information not available	2	Discuss earlier in process	2	28
Drug screen	Chain of custody form not provided	Start date delayed	7	Applicant did not pick up form	3	Reviewed by HR	2	42
	Fail drug test	Offer retracted	10	Applicant drug use	4	Make candidate aware of requirements	9	360

STEP 5, VALIDATE MEASURING SYSTEM

Other performance measures must also be considered. A review of the process map in Figure A.1 indicates that there are important decisions to be made at both the screening of resume step and at the interview step. Questions to answer are, how are resumes evaluated and what criteria are used to decide if the resume is to be sent for further review? What if a good candidate is overlooked or a poor candidate gets through? The next step is, how are the results of the interview evaluated? Are the interviews scored? If so, are scores consistent between interviewers? Is there a measurement system in place or is the decision based on someone's gut feeling?

Many times in processes where decisions have to be made there is no real measurement system. This presents a problem for the next step in the process, which is to validate the measuring system. You may have to develop a measuring system before it can be validated. See the discussion in Chapter 5 under measurement system analysis. In this case, there wasn't a measuring system for either resume screening or interviewing. The team decided to develop a scoring method for both resumes and interviews. The resumes would be scored on a scale of 1 to 5 with 1 being not suitable for the job and 5 being very suitable based on experience and accomplishments listed. The scoring method would then be evaluated using an attribute gage R&R.

The interviews will be scored by rating the interviewees' response to a set of standard questions developed by the team. The questions were designed to get the applicants to explain how they would react to various situations they might encounter should they accept the position. The questions were directed at four areas: teamwork, adaptability, assertiveness, and managing stress. The team defined the scoring system using a scale of 1 to 5 with 5 being the most desired answer. The scale was further defined by listing what points must be made in the response key to receive the given score. For example, a question concerning teamwork that was intended to also gain insight into the employee's attitude was, "Describe an unsuccessful team that you were on. What, if anything, could have been done differently?" For this question, a score of 5 would be given if the team was put in a positive light and recommendations for success were given. On the other hand, if the unsuccessful team was put in a negative light or the failure was blamed on other reasons, the candidate would receive a score of 1. Responses falling between the two extremes would be evaluated and scored by the interviewer accordingly. There will still be subjectivity in this type of system, but much less than in the previous system.

STEP 6, DETERMINE PROCESS CAPABILITY

Once the measuring system is determined to be acceptable, process capability can be evaluated. In this case, the process is measuring using binominal data, that is, the percentage of employee turnover in a year. A p-chart was generated in MINITAB to determine process capability using the turnover data in Table A.2 (see Figure A.2).

The chart indicates a monthly turnover of 2.1% or a yearly rate of 25.2%. This becomes the current capability of the recruiting process to retain employees. The process sigma of the recruiting process can be calculated using the Z transform. If the current rate is 25.3% and the required rate is 10%, there is difference of 15.3%. This would indicate that the process is 15.3% defective. Using the Z

Table A.2 Number of employees leaving by month.

	Termination	Resignation	Total
Jan	1	5	6
Feb	2	3	5
Mar	1	2	3
Apr	3	1	4
May	0	3	3
Jun	3	3	6
Jul	4	4	8
Aug	5	1	6
Sep	4	3	7
Oct	6	2	8
Nov	5	2	7
Dec	3	5	8

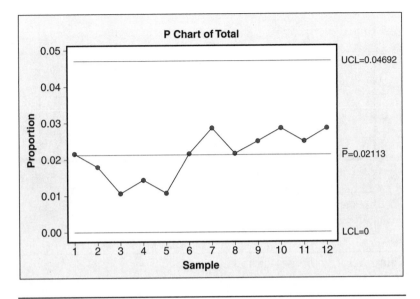

Figure A.2   *p*-chart of turnover.

transform at 84.7% (100 − 15.3), we have a process sigma value of 1.02. The data are considered long-term as they were collected over a one-year period. With data we could report the process sigma at 1.02 long-term or 2.52 short-term. (1.5 + 1.02 = 2.52). The capability measure is used to baseline our performance and evaluate the effect of any changes that are made to the process in the future.

STEP 7, IDENTIFY REASON WHY PERFORMANCE IS NOT ACHIEVED

To determine why the intended performance was not achieved, the turnover data were charted and evaluated. See Figure A.3.

Further investigation into the employees who left can be done using the Pareto chart by looking at the reasons why the employees left. The group decided to break the reasons down by terminations, which is what Figure A.4 shows, and by resignations, which is what Figure A.5 shows. The data indicate that attendance and job performance are the top causes for terminations. Employees who resigned either found a better opportunity or changed occupations.

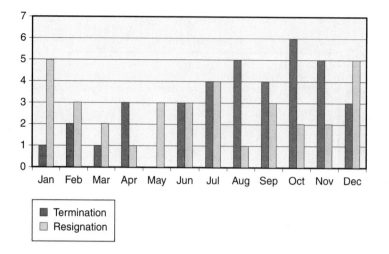

Figure A.3 Employees leaving by month.

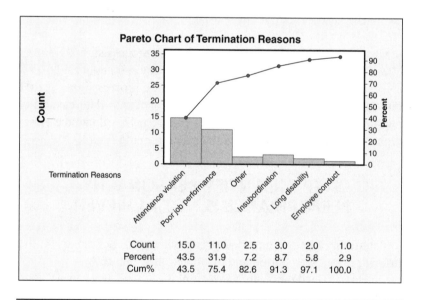

Figure A.4 Pareto chart of termination reasons.

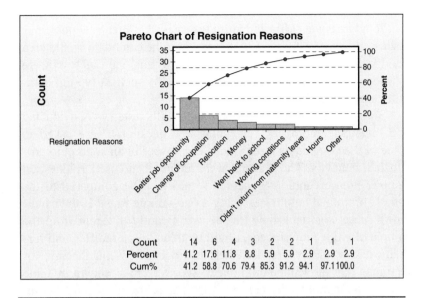

Figure A.5 Pareto chart of resignation reasons.

STEP 8, VERIFY RELATIONSHIPS BETWEEN INPUTS AND OUTPUTS

If we consider that employees are terminated primarily for attendance and job performance, which are outputs of the screening and interview process, we must determine what in the screening and interview process will have a direct effect on our ability to identify those who may have attendance and performance problems before the offer is made. Two major causes for poor performance were identified by the team:

1. Objectives and responsibilities are not clearly defined.

2. Employees are not properly screened for the skills and attitude required for the job.

Objectives and responsibilities were defined and six- and 12-week goals were set for all new positions or replacements for existing positions. The objectives and responsibilities are reviewed with the candidate and are reviewed on the first day of employment with the manager and employee.

To address the skills and attitude issues, the interview questions discussed earlier were used to determine if the candidate would be a good fit for the organization. In addition to this, various tests were developed to assess the candidate's job skills such as typing, computer skills, and math skills.

Both the interview questions and the skills tested were evaluated with existing employees. The interview questions were asked to some of the company's most valued employees in an attempt to profile their behavior. Those scores were recorded and used as a desired sample. Future candidates' scores would then be compared to the sample of valued employees using a one-sample *t*-test. If the candidate's score was determined to be significantly different from the sample of valued employees, it will be treated as a red flag and further work would be required before a decision is made. Say, for example, that the valued employees' scores were as shown in Table A.3 and the candidate's score was 35. The score of 35 can be compared to the sample of valued employees' scores to determine if there is a significant difference.

Using the one-sample *t*-test in MINITAB, the results in Figure A.6 were obtained.

Table A.3 Scores of desired employees.

Employee	Score
Jane	45
Mary	47
Sue	42
John	48
John	43

```
One-Sample T: C3

Test of mu = 35 vs not = 35

Variable N    Mean  StDev SE Mean       95% CI           T      P
C3        5 45.0000 2.5495  1.1402 (41.8344, 48.1656) 8.77 0.001
```

Figure A.6 One-sample *t*-test: C3.

Since the *p*-value is less than 0.05, we conclude that the candidate's score is different from that of the valued employees and would require further evaluation before a decision could be made.

Another validation of the relationship of the interview score to job performance could be performed. That analysis is to compare the interview score to the score the employee received on the six-week performance evaluations. This comparison can be performed using regression analysis based on the data in Table A.4. See Figure A.7 for a fitted line plot.

Figure A.8 shows the MINITAB regression output comparing interview score with performance review score. Ideally the interview score will be a good predictor of the six-week performance score. If not, the interview questions will require review and revision. The sample data indicate that the interview score will explain about 55% of the variation seen in the six-week performance score. These data were generated as an example as sufficient data were not available at the time of this writing.

Table A.4   Interview score versus review score.

Interview Score	Six-Week Review Score
37	36
31	32
43	40
38	39
42	37
41	38
42	39
32	33
31	33
43	39
35	32
45	39
36	40
47	38
40	37

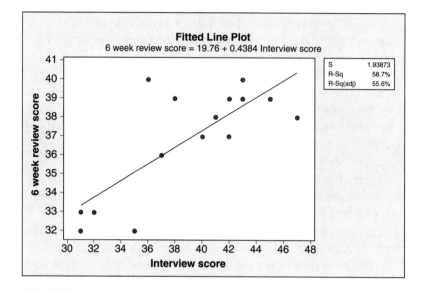

Figure A.7   Fitted line plot.

```
The regression equation is
6 week review score = 19.76 + 0.4384 Interview score


S = 1.93873   R-Sq = 58.7%   R-Sq(adj) = 55.6%


Analysis of Variance

Source       DF      SS       MS       F      P
Regression    1   69.537   69.5373   18.50  0.001
Error        13   48.863    3.7587
Total        14  118.400
```

Figure A.8   Six-week regression output using MINITAB.

STEP 9, CONFIRM RELATIONSHIPS BETWEEN INPUTS AND OUTPUTS WITH DOE AND CONFIRMATION RUNS

Design of experiments (DOE) was not used on this particular project as the major inputs could be evaluated using regression and combinations of factor were not really considered significant. The relationship between the interview score and six-week performance appraisal will be further evaluated and confirmed as more data become available.

Work was also done to determine why people have poor attendance and if those people can be identified before they are hired. This was determined to be addressed through more rigorous reference checking and requiring candidates to release past attendance records.

As of this time, the team has not addressed issues surrounding resignations. There are plans for employee satisfaction surveys to determine if satisfaction levels are related to the resignation rates. In any case, the data would be handled in the same manner as the termination data.

STEP 10, REEVALUATE PROCESS CAPABILITY

In order to determine if improvements have been effective, the process capability must be reevaluated after the changes are made. Turnover data from the most recent three-month period is plotted in Figure A.9.

Although preliminary, the data seem to indicate a reduction in turnover rate from the initial rate of 2.1% per month to the current average of 1.1% per month (in the last three months) or an annualized rate of 13.2%. More data are required to properly evaluate this relationship; however, the results are sufficient to implement changes to the recruiting process.

The results could be compared between the last three-month period before changes were made to the most recent three-month period after the changes using a chi-square table. See MINITAB output in Figure A.10. Note: an average of 284 employees per month was used

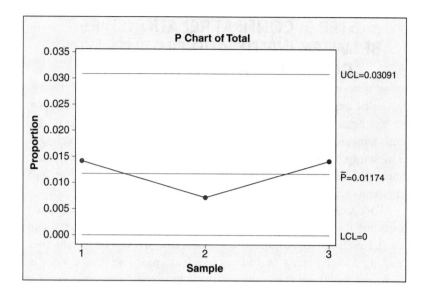

Figure A.9 Employee turnover in three-month period after process improvements.

```
Chi-Square Test: Employees, Departures

Expected counts are printed below observed counts
Chi-Square contributions are printed below expected counts

          Employees  Departures  Total
     1          852          23    875
            858.38        16.62
             0.047         2.446

     2          852          10    862
            845.62        16.38
             0.048         2.483

Total          1704          33   1737

Chi-Sq = 5.024, DF = 1, P-Value = 0.025
```

Figure A.10 Chi-square test: employees, departures.

(284×3 months $= 852$). The p-value indicates that the two periods are statistically different and the most recent period obviously has a lower turnover rate.

STEP 11, CHANGE PROCESS TO REFLECT IMPROVED METHOD

The changes credited with the improvement in turnover rate are:

1. Consistent interview questions with scoring

2. More robust reference checking

3. Definition of job responsibilities and objectives

STEP 12, IMPLEMENT CONTROL PLAN

In order for the findings to be implemented and the changes made permanent, some change must take place in the process. In this case, the change will be documented by a control plan indicating a reaction plan should the required specification be exceeded. See Table A.5.

The items documented in the control plan actually contribute to the original performance metric of employee turnover. The turnover rate must also be tracked to ensure that the efforts continue to have a positive impact on the performance metric. This can be accomplished using a control chart. In this case, since the data are recorded in percentages, the p-chart would be used. See Figure A.11. Once sufficient data are collected, the control limits should be calculated using the most recent post-change data.

Table A.5 Recruiting process control plan.

Process Step	Resource	Characteristic	Specification	Sample Size/ Frequency	Control Method	Reaction Plan
Interview	Interview team	Interview question responses	Total score > 40	100% of applicants	100% verification	If < 40, applicant requires further review by interviewing team
Reference check	HR	Verify past attendance and job performance references	Employee must have good attendance and job performance history	100% of applicants	100% verification via telephone	Job offer will be halted

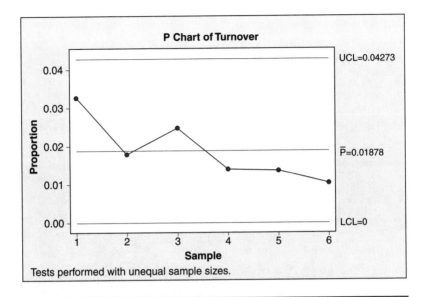

Figure A.11   Employee turnover *p*-chart.

STEP 13, REPORT FINDINGS

As a final step in the project, the findings of the work should be documented and stored in a method that will allow someone who may be involved in the same or a similar process at a later date to retrieve and review the work completed.

Appendix B
MINITAB/Excel Guide

There are many software packages available to perform data analysis. MINITAB and Excel keystrokes are included as they are the ones that I have experience with.

Tool	MINITAB	Excel
Histogram	Graph, Histogram	Tools, Data Analysis, Histogram
Pareto chart	Stat, Quality Tools, Pareto Chart	Bar Chart with occurrence in descending order
Cause and effect	Stat, Quality Tools, Cause and Effect	Create using drawing tools
Scatter diagram	Graph, Scatter plot	Graph, XY scatter
Control charts	Stat, Quality Tools, Control Charts	Templates required
Attribute gage R&R	Stat, Quality Tools, Attribute Agreement Analysis	Templates required
Variable gage R&R	Stat, Quality Tools, Gage Study, Gage R&R Crossed	Templates required

Continued

Continued

Tool	MINITAB	Excel
Process capability	Stat, Quality Tools, Process Capability, then select type of capability	Templates required
Hypothesis testing		
t-tests	Stat, Basic Statistics	Tools, Data Analysis
Correlation	Stat, Basic Statistics	Tools, Data Analysis
ANOVA	Stat, ANOVA	
Regression	Stat, Regression or Stat, Fitted Line Plot	Tools, Data Analysis
Chi-square tables	Stat, tables, cross-tabulation and tables	
Z value to area under curve	Calc, Probability Distribution, Normal (Cumulative Probability, mean = 0, Std Dev =1)	Function NORMDIST
Area under curve to *Z* value	Calc, Probability Distribution, Normal (Inverse Cumulative Probability, mean =0, Std Dev =1)	Function NORMSINV
t-dist value to area under curve	Calc, Probability Distribution, t Cumulative	TDIST
t-dist area under curve to t value	Calc, Probability Distribution, t Inverse Cumulative	TINV
DOE	Stat, DOE, Factorial	Templates Required

Appendix C
Null Hypothesis Table

Test	Null Hypothesis	Alternate Hypothesis
Normality	Is normal	Not normal
t-tests	No difference	Different
Correlation	No correlation	Correlated
Regression	Output not dependent on input	Output dependent on input
ANOVA	No difference	At least one different
DOE	Not significant	Significant

Glossary

accuracy—Characteristic of a measurement that indicates how different a measurement is from the true value.

analysis of variance (ANOVA)—A statistical technique that utilizes variances to determine if there is a difference in the means of sample data.

attribute data—Go/no-go and pass/fail type data. Data expressed in terms of a percentage are typically based on attribute data.

benchmarking—An improvement process that compares current performance to that of another organization considered best in class.

c-chart—Count chart used to monitor the number of occurrences over time.

cause-and-effect diagram—Also called Ishikawa diagram or fishbone chart, used in group settings to determine possible causes of a particular condition.

champion—A business leader that is used as a team resource to remove road blocks and provide resources for the team.

control chart—Chart used to monitor the performance of a process over time by comparing the current samples to past performance using control limits based on expected variation of data.

Cp, Cpk—A measure of process capability for processes measured using continuous data. See Chapter 6.

data—A set of collected facts.

defect—A characteristic that does not conform to an internal or customer requirement.

design of experiments (DOE)—Experimental method by which several input factors are intentionally varied in order to determine the effect on the output or response variable.

failure mode and effects analysis (FMEA)—A procedure used to identify potential failure modes in a process and to prioritize failure modes by occurrence, severity, and detection.

gage repeatability and reproducibility—Evaluation method for a measuring system used to quantify error due to the equipment used (repeatability) and the operator (reproducibility) using the equipment.

histogram—Graphical summary of continuous data created by dividing the range of data into bins of equal length and counting the occurrences of data that fall within a given bin.

input—Information or material that a process requires to produce a product or service.

internal customer—Recipient of the output of an internal process.

out-of-control process—Process that is not predictable based on a known distribution.

Pareto chart—Chart used to identify the critical few causes for a given effect, generated by counting the occurrences of each causes and ranking them in descending order.

Pareto principle—The principle, named after 19th century economist Vilfredo Pareto, suggests that most effects come from relatively few causes; that is, about 80 percent of effects come from about 20 percent of the possible causes.

probability—The likelihood of something occurring.

process—A series of events requiring certain inputs that is designed to produce a particular output.

process capability—A measure of how well a process meets its intended requirement.

process map—A graphical representation of a process that identifies process steps and the input and output required for each step.

quality loss function—A concept describing the nonlinear relationship of the quality level of a product or service to the amount the product or service deviates from its intended target value.

regression analysis—A statistical method that defines the relationship of a continuous input variable to a continuous output variable.

root cause—The fundamental cause of an effect.

Six Sigma—A methodology intended to center a process on target and reduce variation to the lowest possible level.

specification—The requirement that the output of a process must meet.

tolerance—The amount that the output of a process is allowed to vary.

***t*-test**—A statistical test used to determine if a difference exists between the means of two sets of data.

Z transform—Method used to determine the probability that a value will fall into a particular region of the standard normal curve.

Index